Angkor Life

STEPHEN O. MURRAY

BUA
LUANG
BOOKS

Angkor Life

Library of Congress Catalog Card Number 95-078414
International Standard Book Number: 0-942777-15-8
Copyright © 1996 by Stephen O. Murray

Bua Luang Books
2215-R Market St. #FLCC
San Francisco, CA 94114
USA

Floating Lotus Communications Co.
P.O. Box 44
Ratchawithi Post Office
Bangkok 10408 Thailand

Bua Luang Books is an imprint of *Floating Lotus Communications Co. Ltd.*

This edition printed and bound in Thailand
Printed by Pyramid Printers ☎ (02) 712-0199

Photographs © 1993, 1996 by Stephen O. Murray & Keelung Hong
Drawings on page 36 and 51 © 1996 by Gary Bukovnik.
Other line drawings from Beylié (1907), Coedès (1932),
Commission archeologique (1910), and Wheatcroft (1928)
Cover design by Santiphap Chaiyana.
Map 1 & 2, page 5, Map 3, page 6, © 1996 by Santiphap Chaiyana
Map 4, page 7, by Mark Watrous-Heyliger, © 1996 Floating Lotus
First edition 1996

10 9 8 7 6 5 4 3 2 1

IN MEMORY OF

Zhou Daguan 周達觀
who wrote what he saw and was told in 1296-1297.

AND

George Coedès (1886-1969)
who read the stones—and not just those with inscriptions on
them.

Contents

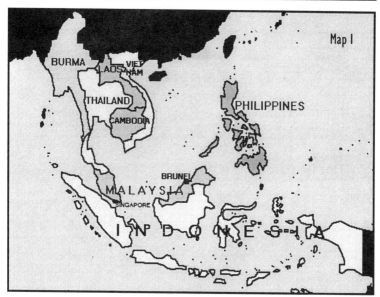

Modern Southeast Asia

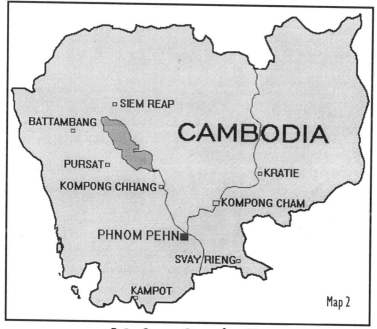

Modern Cambodia

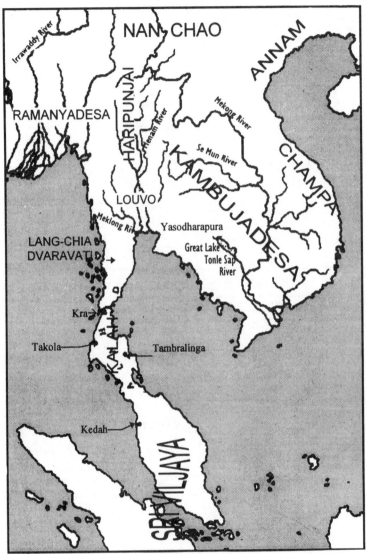

Thirteenth-century Kambujadesa under the reign of
Jayavarman VII.

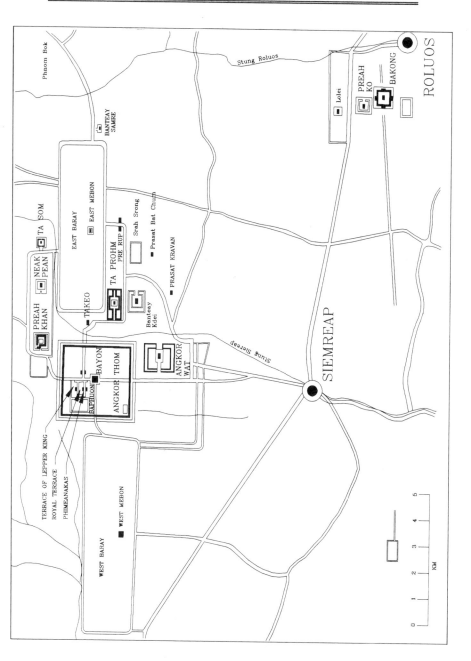

Introduction

After more than a quarter of a century of dreaming about going to Angkor Wat, and long after having given up ever being able to see it for myself, in December of 1993 I was able to visit it and other awe-inspiring Khmer sites.[1] As excellent as the pictures in books are, I had not grasped the extent of the buildings or

Head of Buddhist bodhisattva of mercy, Lokeshvara, at Bayon

---

[1] My enjoyment and understanding were enhanced by seeing these marvels along with Faruq Ahmad, Keelung Hong, and Samnang Pok, profiting by their familiarity (respectively) with South Asian, East Asian, and Khmer iconography, literary traditions, and everyday life. Jean-Luc Hoffer has patiently answered questions I've asked about my understandings of French texts. Keelung Hong and Joe P-Y Kao also helped me in understanding the venerable Chinese ethnologies and in romanizing Chinese terms. They, Jonathan Benthall, and Eric Allyn have pressed for and aided in increasing readability.

of their decoration. I am convinced that the Bayon in particular, as photogenic as it seems to be, resists reduction to photographic plates. Although Angkor Wat seems to me to make more sense in photographs than the Bayon, it also needs to be seen to be believed. Khmer sculptures from the Cambodian National Museum and elsewhere have been very well photographed and discussed in several books. They seemed like old friends when I saw them for the first time—in contrast to the many surprises in the ruins (only one of which was a venomous green snake that Samnang Pok yanked me away from approaching!).

Siem Reap c. 1925

What I couldn't find for sale in Siem Reap or Phnom Penh was anything that told me what life was like in Yashodharapura (Angkor Thom) eight centuries ago, when King Jayavarman VII was maniacally building and conquering, or before. Rashly, I decided that I would write the book that I wanted but couldn't find. This volume aims to supplement readily available guidebooks and the plethora of reproductions of Khmer buildings and art. It is not a history of the Khmer Empire, nor an analysis of its art and architecture.[1] Rather, it is an attempt to summarize what is

---

[1] The bibliography includes a range of interpretations of Khmer history.

known about Angkor-era Khmer society. The main focus is on everyday life.

Although by original training I am a sociologist of religion, and although religion underlay both the florescence of high Khmer civilization and also its later devolution, I have chosen not to discuss it first. I defer discussion of religion and of the bases of everything (certainly including religion)—rice and the water to grow rice—until last. I nonetheless want to foreshadow the last sections by insisting that the Khmers of eight centuries ago treated the kings and the social order as sacred. I further want to stress at the outset that without a rice surplus there would have been no Khmer Empire to discuss. There would have been none of the monuments to visit, and none of the religious and literary elaboration to fascinate later ages.

"Good Spirits" at the south entrance to Angkor Thom

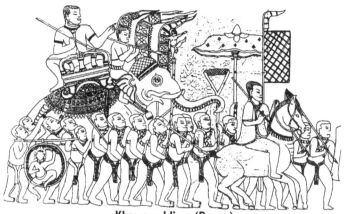

Khmer soldiers (Bayon)

Upon my return from Southeast Asia, I launched a "search and seizure attack" on the stacks of several University of California, Berkeley, libraries. In the shelves of books I hauled away, I found considerable detail about the military and political history of the Khmer Empire. I was disappointed to find much less than I had hoped about its social history. From voluminous French and English translations of myriad Sanskrit and Khmer inscriptions, unfortunately, one can infer practically nothing about daily life.[1] Inscriptions are mostly highly hyperbolic panegyrics to kings or whoever else built the edifice to which they were affixed. All the Cambodian libraries of palm-leaf books perished long ago in the humid ant-ridden climate and in the conflagration of the royal archives when a Siamese (Thai) army sacked Locak in 1594. Most of what we know about life in Angkor Thom comes from a single Chinese eyewitness source, along with

---

[1] Except for land tenure (gift, inheritance, and sale), about which there are abundant texts that do not yield consistent or clear sets of rules, and some accounting of allocation of resources to temples and hospitals.

fragments compiled by two other thirteenth-century Chinese scholars who wrote down what might be of interest to those seeking to trade with various kinds of "barbarians."

Following the review of what we know, or can reasonably infer, about Khmer life during the late-Angkor era, there is a list of kings, an extensive glossary, and an index.

Zhou Daguan Visits the Court of Indravarman III

The Yüan (Mongol) Emperor of China, Timur Khan, grandson and successor of Kublai Khan, sent an embassy to Kambuja (which the Chinese called Zhenla).[1] The Chinese delegation lived in Angkor Thom for a year, from the summer of 1296 to the spring of 1297. One member of that embassy, Zhou Daguan (Chou Ta-Kuan in the older romanization) wrote what he saw there. This single surviving account by a foreign visitor comes from three-quarters of a century after the death of the last and most manic of the builder-kings, Jayavarman VII, whose epic wars and building projects seem to have exhausted the Cambodian people.[2]

Although we must rely on Zhou's notes (supplemented by the scenes of everyday life carved about a century earlier on the walls of the Bayon and Banteay Chhmar, and what little can be gleaned from inscriptions that rarely have much to say about everyday life), basic assumptions about

---

[1] I generally use the modern name "Cambodia" or refer to "the Khmer Empire." Similarly, I refer to "Angkor Thom" rather than "Yashodharapura."

[2] There were no more stone monuments constructed after him, and the last dated Sanskrit inscription corresponds to 1327 A.D. Angkor was overrun and plundered by Ayutthaya troops in 1430. Although he held his coronation at Angkor in 1432, Ponha Yat did not make it his capital. The sequence of kings, with the best estimates of their reigns, is listed in the appendix.

what the Chinese call "Heaven's mandate" to rule legitimately must have been shaken in Kambuja by a series of
military defeats and territorial losses after the death of
Jayavarman VII. A Thai army had occupied much of the
area (though probably not Angkor Thom itself) for a time
during the thirteenth century. However, the then-new war-
rior-king, Indravarman III, who had forced his father-in-law
Jayavarman VIII to abdicate the year before the Yüan embassy arrived, was strong and confident of his destiny.

Zhou heard that, for fear of assassination, Jayavarman
VIII had not ventured outside the palace. Fear of usurpation was probably a stronger motivation, because possession of the palace symbolized legitimate control of the empire as Holy Master of the World (*Vrah Kamraten añ jagat*)
from the center of the universe (the mythical Hindu
Mount Meru). After his daughter stole the golden sword of
state (*preah khan*) and presented it to her husband (rather
than to her brother), Indravarman III had his brother-in-
law, previously the heir apparent, imprisoned and had his
toes cut off.[1] Indravarman III took the further precaution
of having a splinter of sacred iron grafted to him. This
made knives, swords, and spears harmless to him. Thus
magically protected from assassination, he felt safe leaving
the palace (though always with the sword of state—which
some usurper otherwise might seize while he was out of the
palace).[2]

---

[1] Entry to the capital, and probably to any temple, was forbidden to
those without toes. Mutilation was an alternative to executing broth-
ers who otherwise were potential claimants of the throne.

[2] As Heine-Geldern noted, across time in Southeast Asia, equation of
the king and Shiva, "ruler of the country only as possessor of the
empire's Meru, the palace, involved great dangers. It worked as a
constant temptation for would-be usurpers, be it from the royal
families or outsiders, as the occupation of the palace might be
achieved by a *coup-de-main* with relatively small forces and usually
Continued

During his one-year stay in Angkor Thom, Zhou saw four or five royal processions. Soldiers led off, followed by banners and musicians. Three-hundred to five-hundred palace girls carried lit candles (even during the day). They were followed by girls, bearing gold and silver and a dazzling array of ornaments, who were followed by female bodyguards armed with lances and carrying shields. Then came golden chariots drawn by either by horses or goats. Scarlet umbrellas preceded ministers and princes mounted on elephants. At least a hundred royal wives and concubines on palanquins, chariots, or elephants also had golden umbrellas. Finally, the king appeared, standing on an elephant, and carrying the sacred gold sword of his office. The tusks of his elephant were sheathed in gold. Twenty attendants toting white umbrellas with golden shafts accompanied the king.

Continued ⸺⸺⸺⸺⸺⸺⸺⸺

meant the conquest of the whole empire. Many Burmese and Siamese kings therefore were virtual prisoners in their palace, which they did not dare to leave for fear it might be seized by an usurper. The last king of Burma, Thibaw, preferred even to forego the important coronation ritual of the circumambulation of the capital to offering one of his relatives a chance to make himself master of the palace while he was away." The golden sword seems to have been more important than the palace in the Khmer empire. Obviously, it was more portable. The sacred Khmer kings were also less constrained by their sacredness than Japanese emperors (who reigned, but did not rule—except, in some cases, after abdicating).

Usually, he went to a small golden pagoda in front of which was a gold statue of the Buddha. Anyone who saw him en route knelt and touched his or her head to the earth. This prostration is called a *sambah*.

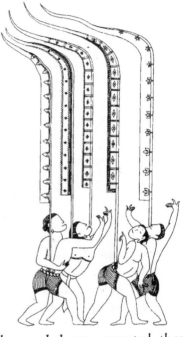

Each day the king gave two audiences at the golden window of the palace.[1] Both officials and ordinary people who wished to petition the king sat on the ground awaiting his appearance. Announced by conch-shell blasts, he arrived on a golden palanquin, bearing the ubiquitous golden sword of state. Two female attendants opened the curtain of the golden window.

All the petitioners present *sambah*ed, raising their heads only when the roar of the conches ceased.

Ma Touan-Lin wrote that the *sambah* was repeated three times. He added that more than a thousand armed guards were present. The king sat on a "lion's" skin.[2] According to Ma, when petitioners or disputants spoke to the king, they

---

1 Ma Touan-Lin said every three days. Although Zhou was on site, not relying on returned traders, the two claims are not necessarily contradictory. The reports synthesized by Ma may have referred to an earlier, less-litigious era.

2 In that there are no lions in Asia (and were not then either), it seems more likely that this refers to a tiger's skin, though it is not impossible that Arab traders carried lions' skins from Africa.

knelt and crossed their arms so that each hand cupped the opposite shoulder.

When he had heard every petitioner, the king returned to the palace. The attendants closed the curtains. All present rose and went their separate ways.

Jurisprudence

Before distinguishing who could wear what, something of what occurred between the opening and closing of the curtains at the palace's golden window might be mentioned.

All legal power was vested personally in the *devaraja* (god-king). Officially, he was incapable of evil.[1] Zhou reported that all disputes, however seemingly minor, were taken to the ruler. He added that the king usually fined whichever party he judged to be in the wrong in disputes brought before him.

Trial by ordeal occurred, including squeezing heads or feet between boards. Zhou mentioned a suspected thief having to plunge his hand in boiling oil (if innocent, it would emerge unharmed). Apparently regularly, the king ordered disputants to go to the stone towers (Towers of the Cord Dancers) across the elephant playing-field from the palace. Each litigant sat for some days in one of the towers, monitored by the families of his adversary. When released, the one in the right would be healthy. The one in the wrong would have been punished by heaven with ulcers, catarrh, or malignant fever. The belief that feeling in the wrong (guilty) will lead to physical symptoms (somatization) continues to be strong in eastern and southeastern Asia.

---

[1] Somewhat cynically, Bechert explained that "the basically Mahayanic concept that identified a king with a Bodhisattva (a future Buddha) meant legitimation of power by a supposed 'posthumous' sainthood without binding the ruler to the rules of saintly conduct" during his reign. This applies to Buddhist kings. Hindu ones were more directly legitimated as divine at their coronation.

The central Angkor Wat tower

Zhou was surprised that the Cambodian king did not have wrongdoers beheaded, strangled, or even whipped.[1] He was even more shocked that there were not serious inquests when corpses were found in the streets of the capital city.

Although the king had ultimate responsibility for upholding order and was the source of all judgment, not every dispute in the whole empire made its way to the palace's golden window. Judges traveled elsewhere. Even in Angkor Thom, there were courts not personally attended by the king. Nonetheless, everything was done in his name. Judges could only make decisions because the king delegated portions from his monopoly of sacred authority.

A body of case law from earlier kings' decisions was available, recorded on palm leaves and, occasionally, carved in stone. The major crimes were murder of a priest, drunkenness, theft, adultery with the wife of one's master, and being an accessory to any of these. Angkor Wat also contains vividly portraits of posthumous punishment of false witnesses, thieves, arsonists, poisoners, gluttons, liars, debtors and adulterers in hell.

Officials and Law

All legitimate power was concentrated in the *devaraja*. His will was administered—and to some degree shaped—by various officials from the royal family or several leading families granted hereditary office (notably the Sivakaivalya family until the reign of Suryavarman I, and then the Saptadevakula family whose members recurrently intermarried with the royal family). The *devaraja* combined the two highest Hindu castes (priests and warriors) and was officially a divinity in human form, not a mortal man. Powerful gurus did more than advise. Sometimes kings gave their

---

[1] Inscriptions record caning as a punishment.

spiritual advisors administrative duties (such as supervising important building projects). Kings also sent gurus on diplomatic missions, and even gave military commands to some.

Civic and military officers constituted an elite above the farmers and the slaves. Their occupations were largely hereditary. Occupational groups were called by the Sanskrit term for caste (*varna*) and performing one's family's occupation well was something of a religious duty. However, the elaborate set of proscriptions and prescriptions that maintain purity and shape life in Hindu South Asia did not operate in Cambodia.

Ma Touan-Lin listed five kinds of officials. He used Chinese characters to approximate the sounds of the Khmer labels rather than translating the Khmer titles.[1] Modern scholars have been unable to make any sense of the terms or to match the sounds to Khmer offices mentioned in inscriptions. My own conjecture is that the terms correspond to the palace division between the chief wife (the *agramahishi*, who lived in the center of the palace) and the four other wives (housed in the four corners). I do not mean to suggest that the officials took orders from the queens, only that the differentiation of officials was based on the same cosmological differentiation, with one primary, and the other four equal to each other, not ranked. The gods of the four cardinal directions *(Maharajikka)* report to the council presided over by Indra on Mount Meru. This was a powerful model—for Thai and Javanese, as well as Cambodian monarchies. Even if, as Ma claimed, he

---

[1] Ma clearly did not understand the principles structuring official ranks, and perhaps did not understand the Khmer terms well enough to translate them into Chinese.

was listing the official titles in order of rank, the five labels clearly do not refer to distinct castes.[1]

A Hindu society not governed by the demands of caste purity is, in a fairly serious sense, not really a Hindu social order. Caste is the organizing principle of South Asian Hindu societies. Although, religious and legal ideas carried in Sanskrit to Southeast Asia were important, the Khmer Empire and other Southeast Asian kingdoms were not governed by Indian codes (the laws of Manus)—or even by codified Khmer laws. The kings issued edicts, some of which were quite detailed. Their edicts were not laws that were binding on their successors. They were only one king's commands. On accession to the throne, a king might have his predecessor's edicts compiled and might reissue them, but there was never a Khmer (nor a Cham[2]) legal code. Various members of the Khmer elite were familiar with Indian legal codes, but customs and the will of the king, not a written body of laws, governed Cambodia.

Although some high officials came from India, the elite was Khmer, not Indian. Cambodia was **never** politically subservient to any Indian state, however great was the cultural debt. As George Coedès summarized:

> There is no evidence whatsoever to indicate that a government run by Indians was ever imposed upon any part of ancient Indochina. The earliest documentation provided by epigraphy records that officials of all grades, with rare exceptions, were native born. All that was imported from India was the administrative

[1] Heine-Geldern claims that because the enthroned king faced east, south (being on his right) was superior to north (on his left) and west (not only behind him, but the direction of death). I do not see any evidence for such a ranking in Cambodia. I think that he extrapolated it from later Thai conceptions to all Southeast Asian monarchs.

[2] From Champa in what is now central Vietnam.

system that had been evolved there through long experience with taxation, corvées, and public works; the carrying out of the system was done by natives. Clear evidence for this lies in the fact that in all the Indianized countries of Indochina the grades of the official hierarchy, like the ranks within the royal family, have vernacular [i.e., Khmer, etc., not Sanskrit] names.

Councils of elders administered villages. Although this pattern parallels India, there is no reason to suppose that it stemmed from India. It has, after all, been common in traditional societies around the world.

While the king appointed governors of provinces (referred to as *praman* or *vishaya* at different times), the governors chose their own staffs. There was no central schools, nor any system of examinations like the Chinese meritocracy.

Dress and Rank

Zhou and other Chinese regarded the Khmer as repellantly dark, coarse, frizzy-haired, and ugly, except for a few noblewomen who mostly kept out of the sun, and thus were (pleasingly to Chinese tastes) as "pale as jade." Both men and women went bare-chested as well as bareheaded and barefoot. Both sexes wore loincloths indoors. When they went out, they wrapped a band of cloth like a *sarong* around their waists. Khmer sculptures show complex pleating and knotting both for women's skirts and men's *sampots*. Men's reached mid-thigh, while

Statue showing a *sampot*

women's reached to their ankles. Elitemen or women might have added a gold or jeweled clasp or belt. These were decorative, not necessary to keep the garment in place.

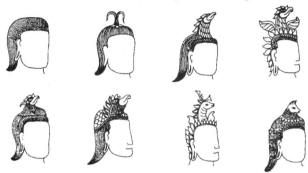

Male hairstyles from Angkor Wat

Elaborate sumptuary laws specified what ranks could wear what materials. Some were woven in Cambodia, but most of the bolts of cotton were imported from the east (Champa) or the west (Siam and India). Only the king could wear *sampots* with a continuous floral design. High officials and priests could wear cloths with recurring groups of flowers. Lower-rank officials and women were permitted to wear material with two groups of flowers.

Occasionally the king would set aside his bejeweled gold diadem and had servants weave fragrant flowers (reminding Zhou of jasmine) into his hair. He wore two kilograms of large pearls around his neck, golden bracelets and rings set with agates on his wrists, ankles, and fingers. The soles of his feet and palms of his hands were stained red with henna, and, as already mentioned, he never left the palace without the sacred gold sword of his office.[1]

---

[1] Ma paints a different picture with the king wearing a white robe, dawn-red cotton cloth that reached his ankles, precious stones in his hair, a bejeweled golden diadem from which pearls hung, golden earrings, leather sandals. (The French translation of Ma adds ivory sandals, but this does not appear in the Chinese version.)

According to Zhou, commoner women wore their hair in a knot *(chignon)* without any visible hairpins or combs.[1] Women of all classes wore gold rings and bracelets. Market-women (and men, including soldiers) in the bas-reliefs have pierced ears without earrings. The elaborate earrings of *apsara/devata* and of kings, gods, and heroes give some idea of what dangled from the ears of elite women and men.

Men as well as women oiled their bodies with a mixture of sandalwood, styrax, musk, dried flowers, yellow cane sugar, and other aromatics. Men, other than the king, were forbidden to dye their palms and soles with henna, although commoner women could.

Apsara (a celestial dancer/angel), Angkor Wat

Zhou wrote that there was a hierarchy of ministers, generals and astronomers, and all sorts of less important

---

[1] The secluded upper-class women may have braided their hair in some of the elaborate ways of the Angkor Wat *apsaras*.

employees (differing only in name from those of China, he reported). These included inspectors, provincial governors, district and village chiefs, superintendents of warehouses, supervisors of corvée labor, and more.

Usually, the king selected princes for high office. Men not of princely rank offered their daughters as royal concubines.

Strict sumptuary laws regulated officials' public insignia and the number of attendants they could have, as well as allowable dress. The highest officials rode in palanquins with golden shafts and four gold-handled umbrellas. The next highest rank had palanquins with gold shafts and two gold-handled umbrellas. The next highest had a single gold-handled umbrella. Lower ones (*ssu-la-ti* in contrast to the *pating*, entitled to one or more gold-handled umbrellas) had palanquins with silver shafts. The umbrellas were made of red Chinese taffeta or oiled (waterproof) green taffeta.

From all over the empire, local officials promptly shipped beautiful young girls to the palace. Zhou was told that there were between three- and five-thousand concubines and palace girls—in addition to the king's five wives. His current favorite dwelled with him as chief wife (*agramahishi*). The other four were distributed to dwellings at each of the cardinal direction (which kept them as far apart from each other as possible). The palace had five pools (*trapeang*), one of which was larger than the others, so perhaps there was one for each of the five royal consorts (and/or for the cosmological principles they embodied).

At least two thousand married woman and men also worked in the palace and lived throughout Angkor Thom. They were recognizable because their foreheads were shaved ("in the manner of the northern people") and they had vermilion marks there and on each temple.

Female figurines (Leper King terrace)

Slaves

"Wild bandits" (*chuang*) captured from the hills were enslaved, along with debtors and war captives. Apparently they understood the Khmer language, rather than learning it, after being brought into Khmer households.[1]

There was no Cambodian coinage. Young and strong slaves could be bought for a hundred *sampot*-sized rectangular pieces of cloth. Zhou wrote that wealthy families owned more than a hundred slaves, less wealthy families ten to twenty. Only the very poor in Angkor Thom had no slaves. It seems likely that in the rest of the country slaves were much less numerous, however.

The slaves remained in their owner's homes, according to Zhou. However, I find it hard to believe that quarrying and transporting stone, mining iron, rowing boats, carrying water, dredging reservoirs and irrigation ditches were not all slaves' work.

An inscription from Preah Khan (the huge temple/mausoleum Jayavarman VII built for his father north of Angkor Thom) listed four nationalities of slaves: Chams, Burmese, Annamites, and Môns from Pegu. Later, Khmers enslaved Thai soldiers, just as the Thais enslaved captured Khmer soldiers.

Slaves could only sit down or lie down beneath the floor of their master's houses (which, then as now, were palm-thatched wooden houses on stilts). When they went up to do their work, they knelt, bowed to the floor, and joined their hands in respect. They called their masters "father" (*patau*) and "mother" (*mi*). According to Zhou, slaves took any beatings without daring to make any movement or sound.

---

[1] Zhou noted that, as in China, there were differences in dialects from place to place. He also reported that the Thai, Khmer, and Cham languages were mutually unintelligible.

Punishments for flight existed, so some must have run away, for. Recaptured slaves had a blue tattoo on their face and might be shackled (arm, leg, and neck)..Inscriptions document that a recaptured slave was punished by having his ears and nose cut off.

Slaves' offspring were also slaves. According to Zhou, it was unheard of for masters to have sexual intercourse with slaves. Moreover, if a horny Chinese merchant had sex with a female slave, her master would not sit in the presence of someone who had so defiled himself.

Male Prostitutes

For slaking Chinese lusts, male prostitutes[1] (in groups of ten or more) were available in the marketplace, according to Zhou. He only mentioned them seeking to attract a Chinese clientele. He did not specify their ethnicity.

Conjugal Duties

The sexual voracity of Khmer women, reported to him by everyone with whom he discussed it, startled Zhou.[2] A day or two after giving birth to a child, the woman was ready for intercourse. In the house where he stayed for a time, Zhou saw for himself that the day after giving birth, a young woman carried her newborn with her to bathe in the river—shockingly divergent from the month's postpar-

---

[1] Literally "two-bodied," but the context of Zhou's censure makes it clear that they were young male prostitutes.

[2] Like twenty-century "professional" ethnographers, Zhou was very interested in the sexuality of the aliens he observed and totally circumspect about mentioning his own sexual conduct. Chinese beliefs that vitality was lost with every "expenditure" of semen, that women were dangerous sources of pollution, and that women should be content with whatever men did or decided for them may explain some of the Chinese shock and concern about Khmer women's freedom of movement, social importance, and (horror!) "lustiness."

tum confinement in China (and in rural Thailand and Taiwan even now).

A wife could discard a husband who did not perform his sexual duties. Wives might tolerate a few days' absence on business. By the tenth day, however, they would seek relief elsewhere, saying, "Am I a ghost that I can be expected to sleep alone?"

However, if a husband caught his wife committing adultery, he could squeeze the feet of the lover between boards. Under this torture, the lover would surrender his possessions to the husband.

Child-rearing

There does not seem to have been formal education except for princes and the hereditary priests (who intermarried with the royal family). The Chinese texts do not mention schools, and there are no Sanskrit inscriptions from schools as there are from hospitals and temples. Inferring from later practices and from the portrayals in the bas-reliefs, it seems that children joined in the work and other activities of adults, learning by watching and trying rather than by listening to instructions given by specialist teachers to groups of children.

Defloration Ceremonies and Weddings

Zhou wrote that rich parents of seven- to nine-year-old daughters and poorer parents of eleven-year-old daughters gave them to Buddhist or Brahmanic priests[1] for *chen-tan*,

---

[1] They were probably Shiva-worshippers. Zhou, in common with other medieval Chinese writers, called them "Taoist." Typically, Theravada Buddhist monks' vows include avoiding any contact with women, even looking at them, let alone deflowering them. Zhou Rugua (whose name used to be romanized as Chau Ju-Kua) distinguished Buddhist priests who wore yellow robes and could marry from ascetics who wore red robes and lived in temples. Attestations of similar

Continued

the defloration ceremony. Each year, astrologers chose a day in the fourth lunar month for the ceremony. Each family with a daughter ready for *chen-tan* notified the authorities and received a candle. The candle was marked with the appropriate hour for the *chen-tan* ceremony. That is, when the candle burned down to that mark the time was right.

The family would already have chosen a priest. The most renowned priests would have been booked early. A rich family would give the priest who performed *chen-tan* wine, rice, silk, betel (areca palm) nuts, and a silver plate worth two- to three-hundred ounces of Chinese money. Less wealthy families would give their daughter's deflowerer presents worth thirty or forty piculs (a Chinese unit of weight). In order to make merit, generous people might contribute to financing a *chen-tan* for poor girls.

A priest could not perform the ceremony for more than one girl per year. Moreover, once he had accepted a fee from a family, he could not agree to initiate a girl from another one.

Before the scheduled night, the family would have erected a platform in front of their house. The platform held up to ten animal and human figures. (These remained on display for a week afterwards.)

The night of the ceremony began with a feast accompanied by music. Shortly before the hour ordained for the ceremony, a procession with palanquins, umbrellas, and music went to fetch the priest and take him to one of two pavilions hung with brightly colored silks. The girl sat waiting in the other. The loud music made it nearly impossible to hear what the priest said to the girl. The priest en-

Continued ————————————————————

ceremonies in mid-twentieth-century Burma perhaps can be extrapolated to augment and clarify (as well as to substantiate) Zhou's account.

tered the maiden's pavilion and deflowered her with his hand. He then dripped her blood into a wine goblet. Parents, relations and celebrating neighbors stained their foreheads with this wine "or even tasted it" (one can feel Zhou shudder). Some Khmer told Zhou that the priest had intercourse with the girl, while others denied it. Chinese could not attend these festivities, so he was not certain of "the exact truth."

At dawn the priest was carried home. He sold the girl back to her family for silk and other fabrics. Otherwise she remained his property forever and could not marry.

Zhou noted from his own observation that after *chen-tan* a girl who had slept in the same room with her parents, no longer did so. Furthermore, after being deflowered, she went wherever she pleased without any restrictions.

Weddings also involved exchanges of textiles. Bride and groom often had had pre-marital intercourse—not any cause for surprise, let alone shame, to the Khmers. Both in ceremony and for gift-giving, the *chen-tan* was more elaborate than weddings.

Ma Touan-Lin passed on traders' reports that gifts by the man preceded weddings. The bride-to-be's family chose the wedding day and conducted her to the groom's home, where the bride's family stayed eight days. After this, the groom received a part of his parents' goods (in lieu of later inheritance) to establish a household of his own.

Given that there was only one night each year for *chen-tan*, there was a great deal of music and crisscrossing of processions of priests going to ceremonies in various houses.

Early and frequent pregnancies made Khmer women age rapidly. Zhou exclaimed that Khmer women of twenty to thirty looked as old as Chinese women of forty to fifty.

Elite Women Intellectuals

Certain elite women, especially in the palace, were able to focus on intellectual and religious pursuits, somewhat as in Heian Japan. Jayavarman VII's mother, Jayarajachudamani, was a patroness of Buddhism. Jayavarman VII built Ta Prohm as a funerary temple for her in the form of Prajñaparamita ("Perfection of Insight," mystic mother of Buddha; this naming is an indication of his increasing identification of himself as a Buddha). His first wife, Jayarajadevi, took in hundreds of abandoned girls, trained, and resettled them. Her older sister, Indradevi provided her Buddhist instruction. Jayarajadevi reputedly could conjure up her husband while he was in exile and later while he was conquering in Champa. The source of instruction in this was not, alas, recorded. After her death, Jayavarman married Indradevi who was "naturally intelligent, scholarly, very pure, and very devoted to her husband." A lecturer in a Buddhist monastery, who was said to surpass the wisdom of all the male philosophers, she was called "chief teacher of the king," an even more signal honor.[1]

Some women had substantial knowledge of astrology and administration. Women held political posts, including serving as judges.

Inheritance and Land Tenure

Ma Touan-Lin wrote that only sons inherited. When a son married, he received goods. If there were unmarried sons when the parents died, they would inherit what the parents left. If all the sons had been married off before the parents died, their remaining possessions went to the public treasury.

Inscriptions also record inheritance by women (particularly sisters of the deceased), however. Not only do inscriptions record inheritance by women, but claims to the throne itself were based on claims to legitimate inheritance through women, most notably in the foundation myth. The kings of Funan, and their successor the kings of Cambodia, supposedly were descendants of a Brahman who married the daughter of the serpent king (naga) of the country. This descent from the daughter of the owner of the Cambodian earth legitimated king's claim to the land (all the land) as his personal property. The most important historical example of female legitimation of a king is the case of Suryavarman I, whose claims to the throne included the royalty of both his mother's and his wife's descent. Rajendravarman's mother was a daughter of Indravarman I (who on his mother's side was himself descended from pre-Angkor kings) and was a nephew of a sister of Yashovarman I and of a sister of Jayavarman IV. Despite hints of matrilineal succession for pre-Hindu sovereigns (and also

---

[1] It is Indradevi's Sanskrit panegyric to her deceased sister from the Phimenakas that has provided historians with most of what we know about the biography of Jayavarman VII.

for high priests), primogeniture was the rule for succession to the throne. Nonetheless, even an eldest son's claim might buttress his claim with allusions to his mother's lineage. After two usurpers had followed his father onto the throne, the man who became Jayavarman VII invoked both sides of his lineage.

If there was a single, coherent set of rules for inheritance, no one has yet figured it out. It seems more likely that somewhat divergent local traditions continued than that any ruler in Angkor Thom promulgated an exact or definitive set of rules to cover all eventualities.

As the Khmer Empire expanded, kings granted lands to those who served them well (one might include gods among those giving good service, since the kings gave them temples along with land to support the temples and their priests). Royal gifts of land and other property transactions tended to be recorded on stone. As Madeleine Giteau noted, "Every text that is concerned with gifts of land from the king to his followers gives the list of the properties thus granted, and the new owners never fail to mention the pious works they have carried out in their new domain: the setting up of images and public works, for the common good."

Land was also frequently bought and sold. As already noted, there was no Khmer imperial coinage, so land was bartered for other goods. Many inscriptions enumerate the purchase price in oxen, water buffalo, luxury objects (including silver vessels and Chinese brocade). Some also record later disputes about payments and/or boundaries that had to be adjudicated by officials (acting in the name of the king, of course).

Funerary Practices

Upon a parent's death, surviving sons shaved their heads and daughters cut away a circle of hair. There was no special mourning garb.[1]

Rather than coffins, dead bodies were laid out on straw matting and covered with cloth. Flags and banners led funeral processions, which were accompanied by music. Fried rice from two platters was scattered along the way from the city to some isolated spot, where the corpse was left. The funeral party returned home once they saw vultures, dogs, and other carrion-eaters arrive.[2]

If the corpse was consumed quickly this was taken as evidence that the dead person had acquired merit during his or her life. If not, misdeeds were presumed to be resulting in punishment.

Zhou reported an increase in cremations, especially among descendants of Chinese. An eroded Bayon bas-relief shows a cremation urn that is attended by princess. Ma Touan-Lin recorded cremation as routine, though also noting that some people took the bodies of the dead to be devoured by savage beasts. He wrote that ashes of the elite were kept in golden urns. Commoners' ashes reposed in multicolor-painted earthenware ones. Zhou also noted that kings' corpses were buried in stupas.[3]

---

[1] This is very un-Chinese, but the Khmer did not wear many clothes, anyway.

[2] A Banteay Chhmar bas-relief shows vultures ready to feed on a human corpse.

[3] Excavations show that bodies were placed in a crouching position, and that the sarcophagi had drainage holes. The latter fact indicates that bodies, not bones were buried.

Bathing

Although concerned about the debilitating dangers of excessive bathing, especially after sex, Zhou saw frequent bathing as necessary, writing:

> Cambodia is an extremely hot country. It is impossible to go through a day without bathing several times. Even at night one often needs a bath or two.
>
> There are no bathhouses, or basins, or pails. Every family, or at least several families together, has a bathing pond. Men and women go naked into the pond. The young stay away when parents or elderly persons are bathing, and elders wait if the young are bathing. Women cup their genitals with their left hand as they enter the water if men are about.[1] Nothing more complicated!

---

[1] He also noted that men and women washed themselves with their left hand. Like South Asians, the Khmers ate with their right hand. They scoffed at (and found disgusting) the Chinese practice of wiping their rear ends with paper after defecating, instead of washing.

Every few days the women of the towns, in groups of three to five, go to the river to bathe. They drop their clothes at the edge of the water, and join thousands of other women already in the water. Even the most noble women think nothing of showing themselves from head to foot to any passerby.

When they have the leisure, Chinese men enjoy the show. Indeed, I have heard that many enter the water to take any opportunities that may present themselves.[1]

More on Chinese Immigrants and Trade

Zhou also wrote that Chinese sailors delighted in not having to wear clothes. "Since rice and such furniture as is used are easily come by, women easily persuaded, houses easily run, and trade easily carried on, a great many dèsert to take up permanent residence in Cambodia," he wrote.

**A market operating in wooden stables
(note the two Chinese merchants at left)**

---

[1] As I have already mentioned, Zhou was very interested in Chinese-Khmer sexual relations, though totally silent about any involvement of his own.

Although earlier Khmers had mistaken the first Chinese men in Cambodia for Buddhas, and revered them appropriately to that belief, Zhou regretted that an increasing number of Khmers "have been learning to outwit the Chinese and doing harm to many who visit."

The Bayon murals show women selling fish and cakes. Zhou confirmed that in Cambodia women were in charge of commerce. Women (specifically, the senior wife if there were more than one) also managed household finances. Chinese newcomers quickly found a mate, marveling that the commercial cunning of Khmer women was as great as their voracious (in the Chinese view) sexual appetite.

Markets were open from dawn until noon. There were no shops or fixed stalls. Instead, each vendor spread her goods on matting on the ground in the space she rented.[1]

For small transactions, barter with rice, cereals and Chinese ceramics occurred. Flower-patterned silks, gold and silver were bartered in bigger deals.

Along with silk and porcelain, Khmers prized quite a range of Chinese exports. These included lacquer, pewter, canvas, mercury, vermilion, sulfur, saltpeter, sandalwood, angelica-root, musk, sulfur, drums, iron pots, copper plates, umbrellas, eel pots, wooden combs, needles, even baskets and mats.[2] The Khmer exported kingfisher feathers,[3]

---

[1] In that the ground was the king's, rent presumably went into the royal treasury.

[2] Zhau Rugua included vinegar among Cambodian imports, though Zhou Daguan specifically stated the Cambodians had no knowledge of it. Chinese writers were specially concerned with international trade and derived much of their information from Chinese merchants.

[3] An imperial Chinese edict of 1107 forbade "depriving living creatures of their life in order to get their plumage for perfectly frivolous purpose" as "unworthy of the kindness extended by the Ancient Rulers to all creatures." Nevertheless, kingfisher feathers were still be-
Continued

(wild) cardamom, (wild) pepper, ivory, rhinoceros horns, rare woods (especially gharu), resin, lacquer-gum (*tzi-kong*), chaulmoogra oil, lucrabau seeds, the skin of ginger root, and beeswax. There was no Khmer commercial fleet and no great inclination for commercial endeavors. Therefore, in the latter days of Angkor and beyond, Chinese traders increasingly dominated commerce in Cambodia.

Roads

Building roads was not a high Khmer priority, either. The major highway connected Angkor and Champa, but there was not one, for instance, to the province of what is now Laos. The few roads that were built were very straight (curving only to hit rivers at an angle). Some were also quite wide (as much as 40 meters wide). However, the roads

do not appear to have been finished. At least, they did not reach any plausible intended destination (neither cities for trade, nor temples for pilgrimage). The roads through areas that flooded during the rainy season had raised causeways. Some bridges (e.g., Spean Thma at Angkor) remain. (Some have been left high and dry as the course of streams has changed since when they were built.) The bridges are piles of laterite, with sandstone naga-heads at each end. The one

Continued ————————————————

ing exported from Southeast Asia to China into the twentieth century. A caged female kingfisher would be used to lure males which were then netted, killed, plucked, and their feathers shipped to China.

across the Spean Praptos at Kompong Kdei is 80 meters long and 14 meters wide. It has eighteen arches.

The roads were not safe, especially at night.[1] Mid-day heat could also be nearly unbearable. Most road users walked, though elephants, oxcarts, palanquins, and horses also moved on them. Zhou wrote that neither horses nor elephants were saddled, but reliefs show elephants with platforms that include railings and roofs. The small Cambodian horses were ridden mostly in the hills, not on the plains.

Rest Houses

A Preah Khan inscription mentioned one-hundred and twenty-one *dharmasalas* (rest houses), fifty-seven on the road from Angkor Thom to Champa, seventeen between Angkor and Phimai, forty-four on the Angkor-Suryaparvata road and one at Suryaparvata, and two at unidentified places. They were built about 12 to 14 kilometers apart.

The *dharmasalas* were 14 to 16 meters long and four to five meters wide. Most were on the north side of roads.

---

[1] Zhou reported that in earlier times the King of Champa received a jar with thousands of gall bladders extracted from living men. The gall bladder was believed to be the seat of courage. The gall usually was drunk mixed with wine. Some of the gall was also poured on the heads of the king's elephants. Collectors who found people walking about at night threw over their heads a hood, and with a small knife removed the gall bladder. The retired official in charge of the collection for the Khmer king lived near the north gate of Angkor Thom when Zhou was there. Reports of gall collecting exist from as late as the mid-nineteenth century (Abbé Bouillevaux).

Their length paralleled the road (mostly east-west). The *dharmasalas* were made of laterite or wood. Most included images of Lokeshvara (Jayavarman VII's favorite *bodhisattva*).

Healthcare

Bas-relief of a hospital (Bayon)

At least in the times of Jayavarman VII, there was universal healthcare in Cambodia. A Ta Prohm inscription listed 102 hospitals,[1] including one outside each gate of Angkor Thom. The hospitals were dedicated to Bhaishajyaguru Vaiduryaprhabha, the healing Buddha carrying shining beryl crystals.[2] Most of the hospitals had moats as well as walls around the complex of buildings. Ruins of some of the stone *prasats* (a tower housing a chapel with a statue of Bhaishajyaguru Vaiduryaprhabha) of hospitals remain. The

---

[1] After invoking Buddha and two bodhisattvas, Surgavairocana and Candravaicrocana, who specialized in healing, the Ta Prohm inscription praises the king (Jayavarman VII) who, among other noble qualities "suffered from the ills of his subject more than from his own, for it is the grief of his people that is the grief of kings, not their own personal griefs."

[2] Bhaishajyaguru Vaiduryaprhabha remains especially popular with Tibetan Buddhists.

Leper King

wooden sickrooms, like dwellings even of the kings, have long ago rotted and disintegrated.[1]

The typical hospital staff included two doctors, two pharmacists, fourteen guards, eight male nurses, and six female nurses. All of these lived in the hospital complex. Outside the complex and working in shifts were one male and two female orderlies for each doctor, two cooks, two rice-pounders, two clerks, and sixty general assistants. Also attached to the hospital were two priests and an astrologer.

Those who lived in the immediate vicinity (all or most of whom worked in the hospital) were exempt from corvée labor, taxes, and even most criminal laws. The sole crime from which they could be punished was infliction of suffering on living creatures.

The pharmacopoeia seems to have been large, but not very specific. Nourishing patients' strength seems to have

---

[1] Stone housed only the gods (or spanned rivers—a godlike aspect of bridges).

been more important than targeting a particular herbal medicine at a specific symptom or disease. Cardamom gathered in forests (rather than being cultivated) was one recurrent ingredient.[1] Other medicines included honey, sesame, clarified butter, cumin, musk, camphor, ginger, oregano, mustard seed, sesame, and sandalwood.

Given the belief that sickness was retribution for sins in previous existences, purification of the soul was at least as important as treatment of the body. As Coedès put it, "The beneficent influence of the Buddhist gods, under whose auspices the hospitals functioned, was worth as much as the medical care or the medicines administered." Building hospitals was politic and at the same accumulated merit for the builder. Something of the scale of the public health service during the reign of Jayavarman VII is indicated by the allocation to it of 11,192 tons of rice per year. It took 838 villages of roughly a hundred inhabitants each to produce rice for the health service.

Zhou Daguan mentioned sorcerers as well as marketplace sellers of herbal medicines. He wrote that the Khmer people cured themselves of many illnesses by plunging into water and repeatedly washing their heads. In his veiw, they overbathed and he attributed leprosy to the horrifying practice of bathing immediately after sexual intercourse.

Lepers were not shunned: they slept and ate among their fellows. No one made any protest, which was surprising to Zhou's expectations that leprosy is a disgrace and that lepers should be segregated.[2]

---

[1] An inscription from Ta Prohm indicates the country's hospitals were allocated 105 kilograms per year, along with 2,124 kilograms of sesame.

[2] A leprous king recurs in Khmer tales. A Bayon relief in which a woman is stretching out what appears to be a noble's "claw-hand" while others massage his right leg, and others hold vases of krabao (*Hydnocarpus anthelminica*) seeds has been interpreted as identifying Jayavarman VII as the leper king. I find it hard to believe that a king

Continued

Nine out of ten cases of dysentery ended in death, he asserted.

Boats

Large boats were made from boards chiseled (not sawed) from hardwood trees. Smaller ones were dugouts (burned and carved out of the trunk of a single tree). The middle of the boat was stretched wider than the ends. Zhou considered the primitive technology of the boat-builders a great waste both of labor and of wood.

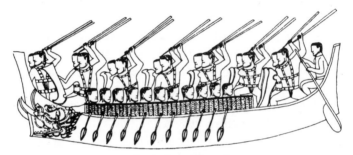

A war boat (Bayon)

Iron nails were used on the large boats. The hulls were covered with chiao (*kajang* in Khmer) leaves held in place by strips of areca wood, and coated with a paste made from fish and mineral lime. Both the large boats (*hsin-na*) and the smaller ones were propelled by oars (*pi-lan*), not by sails.

The Khmer were not seagoers, preferring not even to fish the ocean, let alone travel anywhere on it. The Khmer word *kampong* means a village on the riverbank, not a sea-

Continued —————————————

who vigorously reigned into his late 90s was so afflicted, and do not think he is the patient pictured in this relief. The "Leper King" statue at Angkor Thom is so named because of the lichen now on it. There is nothing to indicate leprosy in the original carving (and I would add that the figure is too slender to represent Jayavarman VII).

port. Indeed, there were no seaports in Cambodia between the annexation/dissolution of Funan (the earlier Hindu non-Khmer kingdom to the southeast of the Khmer and southwest of the Mekong delta) in 627 and the opening of Kompong Som (Sihanoukville) in 1955. Throughout its history, the Cambodian coast has been predominantly peopled by Vietnamese (Chams) and Chinese, not by Khmer.

Angkor Thom is, of course, very far inland. Indeed, it is so far upstream and on such a relatively minor river that it could not be reached with any ease from the sea. The city was not even directly on the river. Surely, this was intentional, whether or not this was a reaction to the ease of naval attacks on Funan.

I do not mean to suggest that the Khmer were afraid of water. They entered *fresh* water with great regularity. They were not oriented outward and (as I already have stressed) they were not very interested in commerce.[1]

Houses and utensils

Houses—even the king's palace in Angkor Thom—were wooden, roofed with palm leaves. There were no saws. Only chisels were used to make planks. The roof thatching was cut at the beginning of the dry season (November) and then soaked in water. Women split each branch and sewed the leaves to bamboo slats. A bamboo trellis was placed on top of the palm leaves to keep the wind from blowing off the leaves.[2]

---

[1] It is hard not to think of the surviving Hinduized outpost of Bali as an analog in both regards.

[2] The elite had tile roofs. The size of their houses was regulated, just as other prerogatives of station were. Zhou wrote that commoners would not dare to use any tile on their roofs.

Houses were individually owned, but fairly empty of furnishings. Zhou noted that the Khmer people buried three stones over which they made a fire to cook food. They cooked outside. Inside their houses they had no stoves, tables, benches, basins, or buckets. The Bayon reliefs also show a man dropping what appears to be grains of rice into a large pot.[1] They prepared rice in an earthenware pot. There might also be another earthenware pan for making

Bas-relief showing containers (Bayon)

---

[1] So far as I can recall, the Bayon bas-reliefs show only men cooking. In late-nineteenth-century Siam Ernest Young observed that "every member of the household knows how to cook." If cooking really had been predominantly men's work, I think that Zhou would have commented, as he did on Khmer women's commercial role and sexual demandingness. Female inheritance (especially hints of matrilineal succession to the throne), a recognized right to sexual desire, the absence of mention of concerns about women "polluting" bathing pools (*trapeang*), and the fact that men took young children along with them as they did their work do suggest that Khmer society was much less patriarchal than Chinese, seemingly frighteningly so to some Chinese male observers.

sauces. Khmer pots were crude and little decorated. (They soon were blackened by cooking fires.) Rice was served on Chinese earthenware or copper plates, while sauces were contained in cups made of leaves. The Khmer also made spoons of chiao (*kajang*) leaves and discarded them after a meal. Serving ladles were made from coconut shells.

They had tin or earthenware bowls to rinse the fingers of their right hand. They did not use chopsticks or other utensils, just their right hand and the leaf spoons.

Common people drank wine from earthenware cups, the nobles from metal goblets. The nobles ate from silver or even from gold plates, and gold utensils graced the royal banquet tables.

The common people slept on rattan mats or directly on the wooden or bamboo floor. The more affluent lay on the skins of tigers, panthers, or deer. Zhou noted a fashion of low beds built by the Chinese. Generally, the floors were not strong enough to support heavy furniture.

Lighting came from beeswax candles or coconut-oil lamps. Some people had mosquito nets. Chinese brocades and embroidered curtains covered the palace walls (as Angkor Wat and Bayon reliefs show).

Eating together was more important than drinking together, public drunkenness being a major punishable offense.[1]

Zhou noted four kinds of fermented beverages, made from honey, sugarcane, rice, and some kind of leaf (*pangyassu*). One of the bas-reliefs at Banteay Chhmar shows an elephant-operated sugarcane press, though Zhou listed this as the least important kind of fermented drink for the Khmers. They made no yeast from grain and do not appear to have distilled any alcoholic beverages.

---

[1] The Arab trader Sulayman, who was in the area in the mid-ninth century, stressed strict prohibition against drunkenness.

Although Zhou did not mention chewing betel nuts as a pastime of common people,[1] it was likely the chief stimulant.

Diet

Rice and fish were, of course, the staple of the Khmer diet (then as now). There were three crops of rice a year. Fish included catfish, shad, gudgeon, featherbacks, some sharks and many eels, clams, prawns—and also turtles. Zhou reported that crocodile belly was quite delicious, and that the Khmer did not eat frogs, which are (I can attest) still very plentiful along the Siem Reap River. Generally, the Khmer did not fish from the sea, but from the rivers and ponds. Salt was necessary for preserving fish, and had to be transported from the coast (where seawater was boiled down or evaporated) or from mountain mines. Lacking barley and beans, they did ·not know how to make soy sauce (and, according to Zhou also lacked vinegar). Al-

Men cooking (Bayon)

---

[1] *Areca catechu* (the tree on which betel nuts grow) is native to the Malay peninsula and Sumatra. Chewing its fruit had diffused to India from peninsular or island Southeast Asia about 2,000 years ago. I do not know of any representation of betel paraphernalia in Khmer carvings before the sixteenth century ("completion" of Angkor Wat bas-reliefs). Zhou mentioned provision of betel nuts to the priests performing the *chen-tan* ceremony and to the spectators of a festival.

though all of them focused particularly on food processing, none of the Chinese sources mentioned fermented fish paste (*prahoc*), widely used in Southeast Asian cuisine now.

As the waters recede at the end of the rainy season, fish are trapped in drying-up ponds, unable to reach the Tonlé Sap.[1] A venerable Khmer observation is that during the flood season the fish eat ants, but during the dry season ants eat fish (that have died as the waters recede). Whether smoked, dried, or sauced, at least some of the fish from the December-January harvest must have been preserved.

The Khmer drank milk from cows and from goats.[2] They ate various kinds of deer, also bananas, coconuts, mangoes, lichees, papayas, and oranges (but not at that time guavas). Along with some palm trees to provide thatch and coconut, some fruit trees grew near houses in the countryside. A Bayon bas-relief shows a man dropping a pig into a large cauldron over a fire. This shows that the Khmers were not vegetarian. Another Bayon relief shows men roasting what appears to be meat that is clasped between tongs rather than skewered. Another shows men using the same technique for roasting whole fish.

Continued ————————————————————

bas-reliefs). Zhou mentioned provision of betel nuts to the priests performing the *chen-tan* ceremony and to the spectators of a festival.

[1] The Tonlé Sap flows into the Mekong about 255 days a year. The Mekong flows into the Tonlé Sap about 100 days with about five days of standstill before each reverse of flow. The Toné Sap lake between Siem Reap and Phnom Penh is 30 miles long and 4 miles wide during the dry season, but swells to a lake nearly 100 miles long from 15 to 40 miles wide during the rainy season.

[2] It is odd that there are no bas-reliefs of milking, especially since this is a common scene in Indian art (often with Krishna). There are Baphuon scenes of hermits using churns, and also an inscription about one who lived on melted butter.

A modern lotus harvester from eastern Bayon

Among the vegetables that Zhou Daguan recognized were onions, mustard, leeks, eggplants, watermelons, squash, cucumbers, and okra. He noted a lack of beets, turnips, lettuce, spinach and chicory. He also acknowledged that he did not know the names for many vegetables that grew in water. Khmers continue to eat lotus pods and roots and the whole of water lilies.

Khmers gathered the honey produced by quite small bees from hollow tree trunks in the forest. They do not seem to have constructed beehives and domesticated bees.

Ma Touan-Lin noted that the Khmer cleaned their teeth with small pieces of poplar wood.

Festivals and Entertainment

No notations for Angkor-era Khmer music survive. Bas-reliefs and inscriptions document drums, gongs, cymbals, tambourines and bells, harps and bamboo guitars. This array of percussion and plucked strings provided music for dancing and background music for accompanying readings from sacred books. Conches were blown to announce him, as noted in the description of the king's procession,

From arrays of gongs and both rounded and triangular harps, it is clear that the Khmer musical scale consisted of seven equal tones.

In the central square between the palace's elephant terrace and the twelve stone towers, New Year[1] fireworks were observed from stands holding more than a thousand persons, lavishly decorated with lanterns and flowers. Every night for two weeks, rockets, as large as swivel-guns, were fired from three to six towers that were more than 50 meters high. Their launching shook the whole city, and people as far as 30 kilometers away could see them. Nobles and officials paid the considerable expenses of torches and betel (areca) nuts, while the rockets and firecrackers, according to Zhou, were expenses of the provinces and noble families.

---

[1] This corresponded to the tenth lunar month of the Chinese calendar.

Dancers

In addition to the great New Year celebration, there was a festival each month. Ball games were the centerpiece of the fourth month celebration. For the fifth month Buddhas from all over the empire were transported to Angkor Thom. The king helped in washing them. The festival of floats was in the sixth month, the burning of new rice for Buddha, the seventh. This burning of some new rice occurred throughout the empire. At Angkor Thom, new rice from outside the south gate was used, according to Zhou. The king watched the festival of floats but not the rice burning. Countless women arrived for the latter, according to Zhou.

The Elephant Terrace at Angkor Thom shows what seems to be a game like polo that was probably played in the central court in front of it.

In the eighth month actors and musicians went to the palace each day for dancing (*ai-lan*). Elephant battles and battles between boars were staged.

A boar fight during the eighth month festival

The ninth month was the time for a census (*ya lieh*) in which the entire population of the empire supposedly was summoned to the capital and passed in review before the palace.

Zhou could not recall the other festivals and admitted that he did not fully understand the Khmer calendar's twelve-plus months. Each seven-day week included two feast days and two days of evil omen.

By the time Jayavarman VII had Preah Khan constructed, there were smaller-scale festivals—or at least breaks from work—on the fifth, eighth, twelfth, fourteenth, and fifteenth day of each half-month. Together with celebration of the new year and eighteen other feast days, there were

135 festivals a year. That is, festivals occurred more frequently than every third day.

Fanning spectators at a ceremony

A Bayon bas-relief shows a cockfight. As in Bali today, cockfighting almost certainly was a popular sport accompanied by vigorous betting. The more refined intellectual pleasures of chess were also experienced (and also are shown on the Bayon and Angkor Wat galleries). Bas-reliefs and free-standing sculptures show acrobats, wrestlers, boxers, and archers. Yashovarman I reputedly could shoot birds with his bow while being carried on his palanquin. An Angkor Wat bas-relief shows archery practice (with wheel-shaped targets held on poles by slaves). Various bas-reliefs also show crossbows. Among the scenes of everyday life in the Bayon reliefs is a man aiming a blowgun at birds in a tree. His companion holds (by their legs) three birds already shot down.

Dancers are widely represented. Stories from the *Mahabharata* and, especially, the *Ramayana* were enacted, as well as being carved onto walls. Bas-reliefs froze various poses and gestures. There was a royal troupe, and also others who performed around the empire for the common people.

Inscriptions from Ta Prohm provide some detail about a spring festival with processions (*pradaksinas*) of banners and umbrellas and male and female dancers that went around the temple three times (clockwise) on two successive days, along with two animal sacrifices and extensive almsgiving.

Hundreds of small ceremonies occurred daily in temples. Priests participated in public processions with the masses. The people did not gather in the temples. They rarely even got so far as the outer galleries. Only a few people could fit in the small chapels inside.[1] Priests lit candles to the gods represented by statues, which were frequently washed with perfumed water. Inside the temples, candles were placed in bronze candelabra and sticks of incense were placed in cups of sand.

Books and Libraries

Pairs of two-story libraries survive at a number of major sites, including Angkor Wat and Preah Kahn. The libraries were not open to any general public. And they contained more than books. One library was used during the waxing of the moon, the other during the waning. Unfortunately, the palm-leaf manuscripts they once contained, along with any on deer-skin, decomposed centuries ago. Only what was carved on stone survives.

From inscriptions it is clear that the royal family and their tutors collected, edited, and copied Sanskrit texts, as well as writing new ones, not infrequently playing with words (punning, etc.). The *Ramayana* was the canonical, most-admired, and best-loved text. The Khmers regarded

---

[1] The Khmer builders lacked the architectural technology to build arches needed to make larger stone-roofed sanctuaries.

Valmiki, its author, as a god. They believed that reading or reciting from the *Ramayana* provided certain spiritual blessings.

Library at Angkor Wat

Destruction of texts was punished with eternal damnation.[1]

Zhou noted that there were professional scribes. He mistakenly denied that there were seals; several have been excavated.

He did not understand how writing without ink was possible. Lines or letters were/are carved in the palm leaves with an instrument called a *so*. Black animal dye poured over the leaf fills the carved troughs, but slides over the smooth surface. The leaves are strung together through holes at both ends. Scenes from the book also might be

---

[1] Books are again protected in Cambodia after the active destruction (and more passive neglect for conservation) of books during the Khmer Rouge years.

carved or painted on the outside of the wooden covers to which the strings attach. The writing is/was read from left to right, top to bottom.

Army

Zhou Daguan was quite unimpressed by the Khmer army, writing, "Soldiers are barefoot and unclothed. Each carries a lance in his right hand, a shield in his left. They lack bows and arrows, slings, missiles, breast-

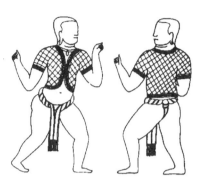

Khmer military garb

plates, and helmets. I have heard that a war with the Thais required universal military service. Generally, these people lack discipline and strategy." Much in this passage seems dubious. Armies without discipline and strategy do not win battles, let alone secure empires!

A battle depicted on ruins at Angkor Thom showing the use of an elephant, with an archer in a saddle

Moreover, Bayon reliefs show Khmer archers, and wearing not only loincloths but tight, short-sleeved jackets (doublets), also worn by infantrymen. Some of the soldiers in the Historical Gallery of Angkor Wat wear breastplates.

The Khmer version of the *Ramayana* (*Ream Ker*), and its representations at Angkor Wat have Rama shooting arrows, not just breaking the bow as in the Indian versions. The army of Suryavarman II shown in the Historical Gallery of Angkor Wat includes archers, and, as already mentioned, another Angkor Wat relief shows archery practice. The Bayon shows elephant-mounted catapults and others on wheels. Zhou seems to have been mistaken about the Khmer army "lacks" that he listed. Even if the Khmer army had degenerated, it is hard to imagine the uses of slings and arrows being forgotten in less than a century.

The iron that the Khmer used came from Phnom Dek (Iron Mountain). Skilled blacksmiths transformed high-grade iron ore into knives, swords, machetes, spear and arrow tips.

What the historical bas-reliefs rarely show is fighting from horse-drawn chariots. These occur only in the mythological representations. Also lacking were firearms. Like the

A war machine (Bayon)

Chinese who invented it, the Khmers used the technology for fireworks, not for guns.

From 1011 an inscription records an oath (in Khmer, not Sanskrit which only priests, not soldiers, knew) of loyalty and service to Suryavarman I in any circumstances and at any time by four-thousand named officers (*tamvrac*). The oath invited every kind of royal punishment for any dereliction of duty, and a curse of being reborn in the 32nd hell for as long as the sun and moon last for failure to keep the oath. It concluded with the hope (not the king's promise) that the king would maintain the religious foundations of the country, that he would provide for the sustenance of their families, and that they would receive the rewards of people devoted to their masters "in this world and the next."

Trying to make sense of diverse religious traditions

It is hard to know what any people at any time believed. In Southeast Asia, as in Taiwan where I have also tried to understand who believes what, people act on what seem logically incompatible beliefs derived from historically distinct religious traditions, some of which have elaborate theologies.[1] I think that, generally, beliefs are compartmentalized. I do not think the elements of most people's beliefs fit together into a single, neat, internally coherent belief system. There is certainly no evidence that what seem like contradictions to outsiders are experienced as contradictions, or cause any discomfort to those living in any society (/cosmology).[2]

Making the complexity more confusing is that it is hard to distinguish those who believe in an idea from those going through the (ritual) motions. Among the latter, some are going through the motions to avoid upsetting others (who seem to them to believe in the rituals). Others (probably more) are taking out some devotional insurance that might pay off even if they don't expect it to.

By the thirteen century (and probably much earlier) there were four distinct and—as long as they were distinct—fairly internally consistent belief systems across Southeast Asia. Buddhism, Hinduism/Brahmanism,[3] traditional

---

[1] See Stephen O. Murray and Keelung Hong, *Taiwanese Culture, Taiwanese Society* (Lanham, MD: University Press of America, 1994), pp. 26-9.

[2] If what some social psychologists call "cognitive dissonance" exists, it doesn't pain most people. It seems to hurt observers more than the observed, and, perhaps, native/observed intellectuals who expect everything to add up and make sense. As Paul Veyne (*Did the Greeks Believe in Their Myths?* Chicago: University of Chicago Press, 1988, p. 84) put it, "The coexistence of contradictory truths in the same mind is a universal fact."

[3] On a continuing "folk Brahman complex" carried with Buddhism and the syncretism of "animism" and Theravada Buddhism, see A. T. Kirsch, "Complexity in the Thai Religious System," *Journal of Asian Studies* 36 (1977), p. 252; Melford E. Spiro, *Buddhism and Society: A Great Tradition and its Burmese Vicissitudes* (Berkeley: University of California Press, 1982); Stanley J. Tambiah, *Buddhism and the Spirit Cults in Northeast Thailand* (New York: Cambridge University Press, 1970) and *The Buddhist Saints of the Forest and the Cult of Amu-*
Continued

Southeast Asian Animism, and simple naturalistic explanations continue to coexist.

As Herbert Phillips wrote of Thailand, "Each of these has certain explanatory functions, but which villagers (often the same individual) also use interchangeably and inconsistently."[1] Neither now nor in the glorious imperial past can one speak of an entity, "the Khmer religion" in the singular. The same is true for "Chinese religion," "Japanese religion," "Taiwanese religion," "Thai religion"— or "American religion." The doctrine of the Trinity, Easter eggs, Christmas presents, Fourth of July fireworks, the stars-and-stripes flag to which allegiance is pledged in schools and before gladiator (football) battles, roving plastic dinosaurs that are venerated by children along with cloth effigies of bears and other animals, and the tooth fairy don't fit together into a single, coherent belief system. No American would try to make all these features of his or her own culture add up. I don't see any reason to suppose that other people operate with tightly logical and consistent cosmologies.[2] We should not be any more surprised that Hindu gods, Buddhas, quasi-divine kings and local spirits (*neak ta*), grand theology, charms, and incantations commingle in Southeast Asian beliefs and practices.

Confucianism has opposed animist "superstitions" (with little success). In contrast, Hinduism (especially Shivaist

Continued ————————————————

lets: *A Study in Charisma, Hagiography, Sectarianism, and Millennial Buddhism* (New York: Cambridge University Press, 1984).

[1] "Some Premises of American Scholarship on Thailand," in J. Fischer (ed.), *Western Values and Southeast Asian Scholarship* (Berkeley: Center for South and Southeast Asian Studies, 1973), p. 71.

[2] I certainly intend to include Muslim societies. The *Qur'an* is supposed to provide a complete plan for life. However, both the profusion of commentaries (schools) and the continued importance of subordinate traditions (of which those of spirit possession are especially common) show that Islam does not provide an exception to this generalization.

cults) and Buddhism (across South, Southeast, and East Asia and on Western Pacific islands such as Japan and Formosa) have coexisted with animistic beliefs and ancestor worship. Indeed, more than coexisted: they have incorporated and fused local gods (not just god-kings) and people to their pantheons.[1]

Most people don't know the history of their beliefs. In Taiwan I found that even temple devotees did not distinguish Buddhist *bodhisattvas* from Taoist gods and deified ancient emperors and generals. A carving of Confucius might stand on the same altar with Lao Tzu, Buddha, and deified Warring States-era generals. Even when (infrequently) they recognize who came from what source, it doesn't much matter to them.[2]

---

[1] Although Buddha and bodhisattvas are not supposed to be gods, they are worshipped as gods in China, Taiwan, Japan, and across Southeast Asia.

[2] Only when I had returned home from Southeast Asia and Taiwan and was writing about what I saw as lack of concern rather than ignorance, did I realize that I didn't know why the church in which I was raised bore the name it did. American Middle Western Protestant iconography is quite minimal compared to Southeast Asian or Taiwanese, but even someone as curious as I have always been, and someone with fairly extensive training in the sociology of religion had not bothered to learn so basic a fact. Moreover, I am not even sure if some of the carvings in my present house are representations of gods, demons, or ordinary people! I don't expect them to affect my destiny. However, some visitors find the masks on my living-room walls frightening. Even the presence of three Guan Yins are not sufficient to reassure some of them.

Khmer religious traditions

The religion of the ruling classes was never unified.
—George Coedès, *The Indianized States of Southeast Asia*, p. 20.

The kings, the court, and the nobility were able to adopt Sivaism, Vishnuism, and Buddhism as an elegant and refined culture; it was not a civilization that penetrated deeply into the masses. Social life there continued on without regard to Manu and the other Brahmanic codes, in contrast to India where Brahmanism was the social order.
—Sylvain Lévi, *L'Inde et le Monde*, p. 121.

Having left the confusing subject of religion for last, and then put it off still further by prefacing it with a general discussion about religious complexity, I must finally plunge into the fusions and syncretisms of the Khmer Empire during the Angkor period. Readers should prepare themselves to read of shifting court allegiances to gods and religions. The basic principles, as stated by two distinguished French scholars in this section's epigrams, should be kept in mind in reading this section. I also want to stress at the outset that as confusing as the shifts described below are, guessing what most Khmer believed at any particular time is even more opaque.

Southeast Asian kings as early as the third century used ideas about the kings being incarnations of Shiva. By the fifth century (Funan times), the Vedic god of the air (Rudra the Terrible) had become the god of fertility. Shiva the cruel destroyer in India, became Shiva the benevolent creator in Southeast Asia.[1] A lingam (an octagonal stone

---

[1] He did keep his third eye in Khmer carvings (though he was more often represented by or as a lingam than in a human-figure statue).

or gold phallus, rounded at the top) represented the king-god's potency. The lingam, called *Maheshvar* (the great Shiva) of the *devaraja* (god-king), was placed in the center of temple-mountains in each capital. The temples represented the mystical Hindu golden Mount Meru, home of the gods and center of the world. Organizing the empire in the image of the universe and the center of the capital in the image of Mount Meru ensured harmony—and reassured Khmers that they were at the magical center of the world.[1] The capital (and, within the capital, the king's palace and the mausoleum-temple in which his remains would be preserved) had great cosmological significance, beyond being the administrative and cultural center of a country.

Shiva lingam

It bears stressing that this cult was primarily Southeast Asian, not Indian. In very selectively taking ideas and customs from South Asia, the Khmers easily forgot what originated where. As Bernard Groslier put it:

> The origins and models were Indian; nonetheless, the Khmers undoubtedly did not necessarily always feel that their culture was Indian, or even trace it back clearly to India. They no longer had direct contact with Indian settlers, who had disappeared, nor, probably, permanent trade with the "mother-country." On the contrary, there is ample evidence that Indian influence—at least by the time of Angkor, from the nineth century onwards—was already entirely assimilated

---

[1] Khmers conceived of the world as square and surrounded by water, so the capitals were square (with each side facing a cardinal direction) and had moats to symbolize the surrounding oceans.

after centuries of Funan, then Chenla [Zhenla] cultures. Direct intercourse was extremely rare. . . . So thoroughly in fact did the Khmers assimilate the Indian universe that for them Shiva or Vishnu were Khmer gods, Mount Meru was in Cambodia, the Ramayana a national epic. . . . For the [common] people, Indian origins were certainly not even surmised. . . .

There are many facts which lead to the conclusion that the Khmers probably chose from the prodigious wealth of Indian culture only those traits which fitted in with their own beliefs and aspirations and only techniques which were adaptable to their environment. For instance, neither the Khmer house on stilts, nor Khmer food were abandoned in favor of the Indian house or diet [or dress or ornamentation]. . . . The Khmer moved forward, and in the course of time modified originally Indian traits. Finally all that was left of Indian prototypes were external forms. The content was quite new.

There was a subcurrent of ancestor worship that is incompatible with belief in reincarnation. Moreover, in the homeland of Hinduism, caste was (and is) far more important than divine kings, whereas rigid and elaborate caste was (and is) largely lacking in Southeast Asia. Hereditary priestly families certainly existed, but they were not Brahman in the full Indian sense. In particular priests were not superior to the king.

The conflation of the Buddhist *bodhisattva*, Lokeshvara, and the *Maheshvar* may also date back to the fifth century. Beginning in the fourth century, Champa kings were attaching the suffix *-varman* ("protector," originally deriving from "armor") to their names.[1] The sixth-century Buddhist king of Funan, Rudravarman, was apparently a Buddhist. Nonetheless, he was careful also to have his lingam worshipped (at Ba Phnom, east of the Mekong).

The founder of the Angkor-period dynasty, Jayavarman II, had spent many years in the ardently Mahayana-Buddhist kingdom of Zabag (the Arab name for a kingdom of the Southern Sea, including Java, Sumatra, and much of the Malay peninsula). In the late-eighth century a Zabag *maharaja* had sent a fleet for the head of a young Khmer (Zhenla) king who had rashly spoken of wishing the Zabag *maharaja* decapitated. It is unclear whether Jayavarman II was in Java at the time, or went there after the Zabag *maharaja* had demonstrated his greater claim to being divinely powerful (and just: he did not despoil the kingdom but only had its king's head removed, embalmed, and returned to Zhenla for the new king to remember). It is fairly certain that the Zabag *maharaja* approved the Khmer council's choice of a new king. It also is fairly certain that Jayavarman II moved inland at least partly from knowing how easily the Zabag fleet had captured the Zhenla capital and taken away his predecessor's head.

Jayavarman II had a Brahman priest consecrate his miraculous lingam on the highest mountain-top of Phnom Kulen (northeast of Angkor) as Parameshvara, i.e., the Supreme Lord, and ratify his capital as being Mahendra, the appropriate place for Shiva to reside. In turn, Jayavarman II made the family of Sivakaivalya the perpetual (hereditary) source of *purohita* (chief priest) and *hotar* (royal chaplain). Priests were involved in choosing later kings, not just in legitimating the winner of contests for the throne. Because the accession of kings was frequently contentious,

---

[1] The suffix was widely used among the Pallavas and other southern and central Indian kings in the third century.

whoever ascended the throne subsequently sought to be divinized by court functionaries.[1]

The Bengal University of Nalanda in Megadha (now Behar) was the theological center of Mahayana Buddhism under the protection of the Pala dynasty (750-1060 A.D.). Shivaist (specifically Pashupata) interpretations of Buddhism, tinged with Tantrik mysticism (that may have revived portions of pre-Aryan northeastern Indian cults), were worked out in Megadha and then were exported throughout insular and peninsular Southeast Asia, particularly to Java. Yashovarman I, who ruled from the vicinity of Roluos in the late nineth century, seems to have been a Shivaist Buddhist influenced by Nalanda syncretism. His successors (notably Jayavarman IV) dedicated temples to Vishnu and Brahma, as well as to Shiva, with whom they continued to be identified by hereditary families of

Roluos group

[1] The French chose Sihanouk in 1941 in consultation with then-still-surviving Brahman functionaries. The Sangha is a Theravada Buddhist parallel organization elsewhere.

priests. Rajendravarman II studied Buddhism intensively. Although he decided to remain a Shivaist, he appointed a Buddhist, Kavindrarimathana, chief minister. Kavindrarimathana built shrines to Buddha and to Shiva. Jayavarman V (son of Rajendravarman II) also remained a devotee of Shiva. He, too, permitted his own chief minister (Kirtipandita) to foster (Mahayana) Buddhist learning and devotion.

By the mid-tenth century, the temple mountains each king built to house the lingam representing his potency were becoming mausoleums after his death. Each new king who reigned long enough to build a temple mountain had his lingam installed in it. After his death his ashes or corpse was deposited there, while his spirit lived on in the image of a god.[1]

Villages were assigned responsibility to provide for the maintenance of temples (not only of reigning kings and their dead ancestors, but of some living men of signal eminence or service, also). Multitudes of Khmer peasants "contributed." Ta Prohm had 3,140 villages with 79,000 individuals working to support it; Preah Khan had 5,324 villages and nearly a hundred thousand persons in its service.

---

[1] In writing about Borododur (the Javanese Angkor) Paul Mus explained that the temple-mausoleum was less a magnificent shelter for the dead than an architectural body, where the magic soul lived on (i.e., shifting from a human body to a stone body). The Mahayanist Buddhism of Jayavarman VII permitted such personal cults. Such self-glorification was anethema to the Thervadist Buddhism of post-Angkor Cambodia.

The entrance to Angkor Thom showing the face of Lokeshvara

There is little reason to suppose the villagers ever saw the temples they supported, even from the outside.[1] Peasants' "tithes"—more likely a higher percentage than ten!—were probably quite unconnected to which god(s) villagers worshipped at home. Villagers were probably more concerned with placating local spirits. We don't know how salient the cult of the god-king (*devaraja*) was for the common people. Most scholars consider that the elite cult was quite far removed from everyday life. *Devaraja* was probably a burden without being felt to be much of an inspiration or blessing to those producing the rice surplus that made a religious elite and royal temple-building possible. Surely the king inspired awe. But it is easy to doubt that worshipping him was very important to very many people at all often. The fertility of wives and fields likely were of more direct and persistent concern!

Although lacking formal religious education (and any provision for access to it), some of the common people who worked as servants and attendants in temples presumably told others about what they saw, and also talked about what they thought what they saw meant. There does seem to have been a popular cult of Ganesha (chief of Shiva's troop, and still a popular figure in Southeast Asia). The elephant-faced god seems to have been a household god for many peasants.

---

[1] French scholars never tire of pointing out that Khmer temples were not products of popular faith like medieval French cathedrals. As I have already noted, interior rooms of Khmer temples were too small for more than a few people to see, so few saw the images of Hindu or Buddhist gods modeled on the kings and members of the royal entourage. In fact, the general Christian populace took no part in the services and only had access to the entryways of abbey churches and to the naves of the great cathedrals (the other three parts of the cross being reserved for clergy; see Georges Duby, *The Age of the Cathedrals*, pp. 247-8).

The Tamil-Malay (Srivijaya) usurper Suryavarman I (who claimed legitimate accession to the throne through his Khmer mother; his father was king of the Buddhist state of Tambralingam on the Malay peninsula) publicly venerated Vishnu, but did nothing to oppose worship of Shiva or Rama. Probably the first Mahayana Buddhist king of the Khmer Empire, he did not interfere with the Hinayana (Theravada) Buddhism and Vishnuism of the Louvo kingdom (Lopburi, now in central Thailand) which he conquered and turned into a province. Indeed inscriptions indicate that he sought wisdom from wise Mahayanists and Hinayanists and at least somewhat disestablished the Sivakaivalya family's hereditary claims to being chief priests (*purohitar*).[1] Suryavarman's posthumous title of Nirvanapada, "the king who has gone to *Nirvana*," is the strongest (though not incontrovertible) evidence that he was Buddhist.

His successor, Udayadityavarman II, restored Shivaism (and especially his own shiva-lingam of gold in the Baphuon), though not the Sivakaivalya priests. Suryavarman II preferred Vishnu, and built what many consider the world's greatest temple, Angkor Wat, in honor of the god he believed himself to incarnate.[2] That is, he was a *vishnuraja* rather than a *devaraja*. He did not fail to be invested

---

[1] Suryavarman began using Sivakaivalyas for secular posts, such as minister of public works.

[2] A surge in Vishnu veneration was not idiosyncratic on the part of Suryavarman II nor was it confined to Cambodia. As Coedès wrote (in *Indianized States*, p. 162):

This fervor for a cult that was more capable than Sivaism of inspiring devotion (*bhakti*), the mystic pouring out of the soul toward the divinity, is found in the same period in Java, where the kings of Kadiri all represented themselves as incarnations of Vishnu. It is also synchronous with the religious movement that in India, at the beginning of the twelfth century, inspired Ramanuja, the founder of modern Vishnuism.

in proper Shivaist fashion but, like Suryavarman I, he did not have statues of Shiva built in his image. And, also like Suryavarman I, the posthumous name of Suryavarman II, Paramavishnuloka, signifies his ultimate allegiance: in his case to Vishnu.

After several decades of near-anarchy, culminating in a Cham invasion and the decapitation of a usurper king, Jayavarman VII took over in 1177 and repelled the Chams. [1] Although he had spent much of his adult life studying Buddhism, and had chosen voluntary exile in Champa rather than shed blood contesting the usurpation of the Khmer throne after the death of his father Dharanindravarman II in 1160 or another usurpation in 1165 (at which time he returned), he proved himself a ruthless general and (very un-Khmer-like!) a great admiral. He not only liberated his country from Champa, but crushed it in 1190. The bas-reliefs of the Bayon and Banteay Chhmar[2] celebrated his victory over the Chams. In that (as seems likely) Jayavarman VII's was the model for Lokeshvara's, each of the hundreds of towers repeats his visage looking in each cardinal direction. Presumably, considerable Cham slave labor built these gigantic edifices and many of his other epic building projects (Preah Khan, Ta Prohm, Banteay Kdei, the seven- to eight-meter-high walls around Angkor Thom, roads, hospitals, and so on). The scale of his taking of lives and of his self-aggrandizement as military liberator of his people make Jayavarman VII seem rather

---

[1] He postponed his investiture as *devaraja* until 1181, by which time he had restored order to a land that had been "heavy with crimes."

[2] Built northwest of Angkor, and long inaccessible on the Cambodia-Thailand border, Banteay Chhmar dwarfed Angkor Wat. Its central mass is 40 x 200 meters in contrast to Angkor Wat's 60 x 60. Thus, Banteay Chhmar is the largest temple in the world.

un-Buddhist.[1] Twentieth-century historians have labeled him a "megalomaniac" and blamed him for exhausting the Khmer people in a final burst of warring and building. His fervor, both as a Khmer nationalist (imperialist) and as a devotee of Lokeshvara are not open to question. As Suryavarman II was a *vishnuraja,* Jayavarman VII was a *buddharaja.* A Preah Khan inscription records the installation around the empire of 23 images of Jayabuddhamahanatha, i.e., the king Jaya-Buddha-great savior (*mahanatha*). In his funerary temple, the Bayon (built on the site of the temple of his predecessor Buddhist monarch, Suryavarman II), Jayavarman VII installed a gigantic stone Buddha Amitabha statue (rediscovered in 1930s under the central tower, where a *devaraja*'s lingam would usually have been). The posthumous name of Jayavarman VII, Mahaparamasaugata, means "great and supreme Buddha," a name perfectly in keeping with his humility.

Despite his commitment to Mahayanist Buddhism, there is no record of his having tried in any way to suppress other religious devotions anywhere in what was, by his conquests, the largest Khmer Empire ever. Nor is there any evidence of strife between cults during his reign. His kingdom needed the protection of terrestrial gods worshipped by his ancestors, although they were not the path to ultimate enlightenment *(nirvana).* Hindu ceremonies continued to be performed by the Brahman priests, as they had been for his non-Buddhist predecessors. In turn, Brahmans continued to be respected and supported by the state. Jayavarman VII appointed Hrishikesha, a Brahman guru from Burma *purohita* (chief priest), a post he retained under two of Jayavarman VII's successors. Jayavarman VII

---

[1] So is the inscription commemorating his marriage to the capital city (that was not just adorned with jewels and nobly-born, but "burning with desire" for him) in order "to procreate good fortune for his people."

did not in any way suppress the Shivaism of his predecessor and successor kings. Indeed, the dance of Shiva, the sleep of Vishnu, the exploits of Rama and Krishna, as well as representations of *bodhisattva*s and the life of Buddha decorate his buildings. Respect for his ancestors (not least as a precedent for his successors whom he beseeched to maintain what he built) required that he maintain the temples that his royal predecessors had built.[1]

Jayavarman VII c. 1200

I find it hard not to interpret Jayavarman VII's construction of gigantic funerary temples to both his deified parents (Preah Khan for his father deified as Lokeshvara and Ta Prohm for his mother deified as Prajñaparamita) and a deceased son (Banteay Chhmar) as a form of ancestor worship (they constitute at least a cult of his family). Ancestor worship may well have been more comprehen-

---

[1] A possibly pre-Hindu stratum of ancestor worship is common in Southeast Asia (and, of course, prevalent in "traditional Chinese culture"). A not-fully-articulated ancestor worship complex seems to me to undercut full belief in reincarnation and also in the attractiveness of a bodiless existence (*nirvana*) for Southeast Asians.

sible to Khmer commoners than either the Vishnu-Shiva syncretism (as Harihara) or the far-from-selfless Buddhism of Jayavarman VII.

Unrecognized as a threat bearing down on the Cambodian Empire during the reign of Jayavarman, was a Buddhism less compatible with a *buddharaja* demanding much of his people (as ostentatious as Jayavarman VII's compassion and identification with Lokeshvara were). A major Singhalese (Sri Lankan) invasion of Pagan in 1164-1165 (not unrelated to the suppression of Hinayanist Buddhism in southern India in the mid-twelfth century) led to the establishment of Hinayanism among the Burmese in the latter years of the twelfth century. Hinayanism spread into the Khmer Empire, especially through Louvo: the semi-Khmerized Môns of the lower Menan valley had been Hinayanists for centuries.

Harihara (showing the division of Shiva and Vishnu)

If Jayavarman VII exhausted the Khmer, it must have been the maintenance rather than the construction of his buildings, and the maintenance of the staff of priests and attendants. The Khmer Empire did not collapse quickly. The successors of Jayavarman VII returned to Shivaist orthodoxy, and unleashed an orgy of vandalizing images of Buddha bequeathed by him on his way to *nirvana*.[1] The last Sanskrit inscription (from 1327, thirteen years before Angkor Thom was sacked by Ayutthaya) written by a

---

[1] Coedès suggests a simpler motive than systematic iconoclasm: greed. That is, in searching for gold and jewels, pillagers knocked over statues, broke pedestals, tore up floors, etc.

Brahman priest named Vidyeshadhimant, was thoroughly Shivaist. (Shindravarman composed the first (surviving) Pali inscription in 1309, after his abdication.)

Zhou Daguan is little help in gauging the popularity among the people of the three religions about which he wrote. He was unable to learn what the *pandits* (Brahman priests) worshipped. They had no schools or seminaries, and he found it equally difficult to know what books they read. (One has to wonder if he thought of asking!) The *pandits* dressed like other (common) men, except for a white ribbon (pre-

Cobra-hooded Buddha, Louvu era, Thailand

sumably the *upavita*, the Brahmanic cord) they wore around the neck for their whole lives. This marked them as lettered; that is, they were literate in Sanskrit; they were not necessarily "literati," even part time. Those who entered the king's service could reach the highest positions.

The (Hinayanist) monks (*chu-ku*) shaved their heads, wore yellow robes, leaving one shoulder bare. For the lower part of their body they wore a yellow strip of cloth. They went barefoot. Some temples had tile roofs. (Others must have been thatched.) Temples contained but one vermilion and blue clay image, closely resembling the Buddha Sakyamuni. They called it *Pol-lai* (= *Preah*). The image was draped in red. Buddhas on the towers were all different and all bronze. No bells, drums, cymbals, or banners were in evidence.

According to Zhou, all the *chuku* ate meat and fish, but they did not drink wine. They also offered fish and meat to the Buddha. The *chuku* ate one meal a day, donated by a patron. There were no cooking facilities in the temples.

The books from which they recited were "very numerous," Zhou wrote. These were made of neatly bound palm-leaves covered with black writing.

Some of the *chuku* were royal counselors, and (therefore) had the right to be conveyed in palanquins with gold shafts accompanied by umbrellas with gold or silver handles. There were no Buddhist nuns.

The *pa-sseu-wei* (presumably Shivaists, possibly of the Pashupata sect, though labeled "Taoist" by medieval Chinese writers including Zhou Daguan), like the pandits, dressed as men of the people, except for wearing a white or red headcloth like the *ku-ku* of Mongol women, but worn a little lower. Like the Buddhists, they had tile-roofed ashrams, albeit smaller ones, for they had not achieved the prosperity of the Buddhists.

Zhou interpreted the blocks of stones (lingam) that the Khmers worshipped as being analogous to the Chinese Earth God altars.[1] He noted that there were no nuns. The priests did not share the food of other people and did not eat in public, nor did they drink wine. As also for the pandits, Zhou did not know what sacred texts this religion was based upon. He commented that he was never present at

---

[1] Similarly, some Christian missionaries in Africa and the Americas found some "heathen" rites as containing distorted or forgotten fragments of what they considered the one True Religion.

readings of their holy books, nor did he observe them making merit by doing anything for others.

Some children of the laity were attached to the priests for instruction. After they grew up, they returned to the laity (that is novices did not necessarily become priests).

Alas for those of us who would like to know more about who worshipped what in Angkor Thom, Zhou's section on religion ends with the laconic statement, "I was not able to investigate all this in detail."

He did not write anything about forest ascetics (*rishi*), who appear in many surviving carvings, both alone, and in ashrams with circles of disciples listening to them impart wisdom (some times in response to questions). Aside from lecturing their disciples and answering their questions, *rishi* had to tend a fire into which milk was sacrificed at sunrise and just after sunset. *Rishi* are shown feeding cows, churning butter, and gathering plants and roots, so they did not depend upon alms. Since ani-

**Head of a *rishi* (forest ascetic), c. 1000.
[National Museum]**

mals could not be killed in the vicinity of ashrams, they are shown looking quite safe and confident in the presence of *rishi*.

Readers may feel that I have examined the waves of Mahayanist, Shivaist, and Vishnuist ascendancy in too much detail, especially since the great Hinayanist wave building at the ime of Jayavarman VII flooded all of Southeast Asia, everywhere eroding the ideological warrant for the civilization of the *devaraja*. However, without royal cults of deified kings (along with a rice surplus), the great Khmer monuments that inspired writing and reading this book would not have been built. Their construction and maintenance were probably much more of a burden than a cause of pride or celebration for most of the Khmer people of the Angkor era,[1] and became increasingly so as the progressive loss of territory in the contracting empire left fewer and fewer peasants to support the existing temples, roads, and other public works (including the irrigation structures). Hinayana Buddhism clearly was a relief from the burdens of the glory of Sanskrit-writing priests and the monarchs they deified. Between the Hinayanist erosion and the depredations of increasingly bellicose Thais, the Angkor civilization devolved, and after Thais sacked Angkor Thom, Khmer kings abandoned the city.[2]

As Louis Finot suggested in 1908:

---

[1] Staffing listed in inscriptions strains belief. For instance, 444 chefs, 4,606 servants, 2,298 serving girls (a thousand of whom were dancers) at Preah Khan, 2,740 officiants and 2,232 assistants (615 of whom were dancing girls) at Ta Prohm. These are not round numbers of any obvious metaphorical (or rhetorical) weight, but can they really have described existing staffing at any time?

[2] Angkor Wat was never abandoned. It was maintained as a Hinayanist monastery, and has become the symbol of the glorious past for modern Khmer nationalists of all sorts, even the odious mass-murderers of Pol Pot's "Khmer Rouge."

There is no evidence that the Khmer people resisted the Thai aggression with vigor. They perhaps even looked on it as a deliverance. They had been

"Leper King" terrace, unfinished reliefs

forced not only to supply the labor to construct immense monuments, the size of which still staggers us, but to maintain innumerable temples [in which they could not worship]. . . . They did not defend these rapacious gods or the slave-drivers and tithe-collectors with much ardor. The conqueror, in contrast, offered them a gentle religion of resignation, well suited to exhausted and discouraged people, and demanding far less: its ministers were pledged to poverty, content with alms of rice. This moral religion stressed peace of the soul and social harmony. We can understand why the Khmer people readily accepted it and happily put aside the burden of their former glory.

Irrigation

The great Khmer monuments that made me (and, in all likelihood, you) wonder what life was like in the empire that built them could not have been built without a surplus of rice and the increase in population made possible by multiple harvests of rice. The supply of water was the foundation of the Khmer Empire. (The same can—and has—been said for many other Asian and Western Pacific polities.) Agricultural bounty was proof of heaven's favor. Before leaving the realm of religion to detail the mechanics of rice-growing, I would like to quote the judgment of Bernard Groslier:

The fundamental Khmer religion, under its brilliant Indian cloak, was the cult of waters and the soil. As master of the earth, the god-king regulated the water. . . . The *naga* god of the waters [represented as a snake] was the central figure of the popular religion.

A young monk in the Angkor Wat main entrance

Rainfall seems considerable. Over the course of an average year, 1,500 mm of rain fall. It rains on about a hundred days, mostly during the southwest monsoon season lasting from May to early October. However, this rainfall is not sufficient for more than one annual crop of rice. Wet-rice (*oryza sativa*) needs a lot of water to grow. Moreover, the Southeast Asian soil needs to be replenished with floodwaters. Iron-oxide buildups also need to be washed away. The Mekong River floods and does these things on a stupendous scale. The Siem Reap River also does them, though on a much smaller scale. The soil around Angkor is relatively poor and easily depleted.[1]

Earthen dams and dikes contained and channeled water. The reservoirs were, in effect, gravity-feed tanks. That is, the water was stored where, when released, it would flow down into canals and fields.[2] Wooden sluice gates released water as needed.

The scale and complexity of water management in the Khmer Empire are impressive, even now. However, there, as in other fallen empires, no one understood the importance of its forests and their relationship to rainfall and soil conservation. More and more land was deforested to be turned into rice paddies. The rice harvests supported the temples[3] that called down the rain that grew the rice that fed more

---

[1] North of where the Great Lake floods, the population density in the late nineteenth century was only about six persons per square mile. Rice-growing regions of northern Vietnam and Java then supported more than a hundred times as many people.

[2] In contrast, Indian temples had tanks from which water could be drawn, or lifted by water-wheels.

[3] About a sixth of land newly brought under cultivation belonged to a temple responsible for the prosperity of adjacent land owned by farmers. Besides working the temple fields, the farmers also had to pay taxes in rice to the government, and perform corvée labor. Although land was bought and sold often, its obligations to kings and temples remained the same,

people who cleared more land and built more temples . . . On and on, progress charged. The way I have phrased this already signals my belief that "progress" was something of an illusion. Soil sterilization and desertification are dangers from extensive/intensive irrigation. Although not as obviously as in some other places, clearing forests for agricultural use led to a decrease in rainfall in Cambodia, particularly in the Siem Reap watershed. Iron oxide built up, especially in fields flooded only by irrigation.

The immediate and most obvious case for the abandonment of Angkor Thom was its vulnerability to increasingly aggressive Thai raids. Incipient desertification was not understood at the time. It also has been considered less in explanations for the fall of Angkor than for the devolution of other civilizations, including the Maya, perhaps its closest companion, another locale with seemingly heavy tropical rainfall. Nonetheless, there is reason to suppose that if the Khmer Empire had remained at peace longer, it would have faced increasingly serious ecological stresses. However, as any visitor to the ruins knows, rather than becoming a desert, the jungle returned—not just to the rice fields, but to the capital city itself.

The Major Waterworks

Although, in a long run, urban civilization on the Siem Reap River did not remain viable, Khmer waterworks were very impressive feats of engineering and construction. Given that the society rested on them, I want to mention construction of some of the most important ones. (See Map 4, page 7.)

Within five days of his coronation in 877, Indravarman began construction of the **Indratataka**. This was the first of the immense reservoirs in the Angkor region. It was north of his capital, Hariharalaya (centered on the Bakong). Indravarman's son, Yashovarman, built the four brick towers of what is now called Lolei, the northernmost of the "Roluos group," on an island in the Indratataka as a memorial to Indravarman and his other ancestors.[1]

Yashovarman also moved his capital northwest from the Roluos area. Emulating—or competing with—his father, he had the **Yashodharatataka (Eastern Baray)** dug and surrounded by earthen levees. It was 1.8 by 7 kilometers.[2] Full, it would have held 30 million cubic meters of water. He also had the natural course of the Siem Reap river "corrected." Slaves channeled it to run west of the northern dike and then along the west side of the Yashodharatataka.

Yashovarman's engineers also constructed an elaborate system of water-storage tanks and canals for his capital (around Phnom Bakheng).

Jayavarman IV had the **Rahal**, a reservoir 360 x 1,200 meters, built in a tributary of the Siem Reap southeast of Prasat Thom.

Either Udayadityavarman II or Suryavarman I had dug the hugest of all Khmer reservoirs—2.2 by 8 kilometers.[3] Full, it would have held 40 million cubic meters of water. Its eastern dike is a kilometer west of the western wall of Angkor Thom. The sites of some earlier capitals were at the western end of this massive reservoir. Although the eastern part of it silted up centuries ago, the western part of the

---

[1] The Indratataka silted up and has not held water for close to a millennium.

[2] On the southern bank, Yashovarman endowed construction of an eclectic set of one hundred ashrams for various Hindu sects, and possibly also a Buddhist one. The temple in the middle, i.e., the Eastern Mebon was built in 952 by Yashovarman's nephew and successor Rajendravarman.

[3] Unlike for the Eastern Baray, archaeologists found no inscriptions from the dedication of the Western Baray. Thus, we do not know what it was called. (Suryatataka seems most likely to me.) The temple (the Western Mebon) is in Baphuon style. However, as the examples in this section have shown, the temples in the reservoirs tended to be built later than the time of construction of the reservoirs themselves.

Western Baray, still contains water. The Western Baray is bigger than Yashovarman's Yashodharatataka (Eastern Baray), which was drying up. On a small island in the middle of the reservoir a temple consecrated to Vishnu was built. It housed a six-meter-long bronze statue of a Vishnu resting on the waters of the earth. (The surviving upper part of this sublime masterpiece can now be seen in the National Museum in Phnom Penh.)

Reclining Vishnu (bronze), c. 1050-1100 [National Museum].
Fragment from Western Nebon.

During the reign of Suryavarman I, a system of thousands of inter-connected brick cisterns, ponds, and fountains was built. Some are as large as 14 by 100 meters. Although some were connected to the Siem Reap River, others depended upon collecting rainwater. Some provided drinking water. Others were fishponds. Most were used for bathing (see the section above on bathing).

Somewhat surprisingly (given his megalomania and the general giantism of his building projects), Jayavarman VII did not construct the largest *baray*. The **Jayatataka** (North Baray), just west of Preah Khan, is 900 by 3,700 meters, only half the size of the East Baray. What it lacked in (relative) size, Jayavarman VII made up for in grandiosity of claims for the holiness of its waters. Dedicated to Buddha (and later to Lokeshvara), it was treated as the Lake Anatavtpa, the legendary Himalayan source of the four great rivers of the world, which also is supposed to be the last place to dry up at the end of the present *kalpa* (cosmic period). Stone spouts (as usual, in the cardinal directions) of the heads of a man, a lion, a horse, and an elephant represented the rivers. The Jayatataka water was believed to wash away sins. Ritual bathing centered on the island temple, Neak Pean. Water from the Jayatataka poured across lingams as it flowed into Neak Pean's bathing pools.

With its construction, the capital had gigantic reservoirs dedicated to Shiva (the East Baray), Vishnu (the West Baray), and Buddha (the North Baray). This well illustrates the multiple legitimations of the Khmer kings.

Rice Growing and Peasant Exhaustion

The 75 million cubic meters of water in the three barays irrigated three annual rice crops in an area of about 1,000 square kilometers. In that rice takes about five months to grow from seed, three annual crops required growing seedlings in seedbeds and then transplanting the seedlings to rice paddies when they were 20 to 25 centimeters in height. Although very labor-intensive, transplanting made it possible to start one crop two or more weeks before harvesting an earlier one. It has been estimated that the district irrigated from the Angkor barays yielded two to 2.5 metric tons of rice per hectare annually. If half the 1,000-square-kilometer area was under cultivation (which seems a fairly conservative estimate) about 140 (±10) metric tons of rice were produced each year.[1]

---

[1] Without manure—to the astonishment of Chinese.

Transplanting rice seedlings to fields plowed by water buffaloes in the Khmer Empire differed hardly at all from how it is done now in Cambodia. Similarly, harvesting with metal sickles, separating the chaff from the grain by tossing basketsful in the air can be watched today. Even oxcarts have only partially been replaced by motorized transport to granaries and markets.

How much rice went to building and maintaining temples and successive kings' other (and increasingly grandiose) projects is unclear. It seems very likely that by the thirteenth century some degradation of soil quality led to some drop in productivity. The Khmer army was also decreasingly able to protect the empire's granaries from Thai and Cham raids. Farmers, thus, likely were squeezed harder and harder. They well may have been relieved by the abandonment of imperial glory in general, and of Angkor Thom in particular, as Finot suggested (quoted above).

The Khmer Empire did not fall all at once, as dramatic as was Ayutthaya's sack of Angkor Thom in 1430-1431. Various projects begun more than a century earlier (including not only the Bayon bas-reliefs, but the earlier ones of Angkor Wat) were never finished. Revenues and supplies of slave labor dwindled. Hinayana monks and temples asked for alms instead of demanding support as Mahayanist, Shivaist, and Vishnu priests had. Hinayana Buddhism un-deified the Mahayana Buddha and his *bodhisattvas*, including any kings considering themselves to be *buddharajas*. Hinayana Buddhism provided no legitimation of deifying kings or of pursuing earthly glory, especially any that involved the taking of lives. Not only maintaining the Hindu temples,[1] but even working in one's

---

[1] Fortunately for the world's cultural heritage, Angkor Wat became a Hinayana Buddhist monastery and pilgrimage site for Thais and
Continued

occupation or working with fellow villagers on maintaining irrigation dikes lost their religious warrant. The popular religion radically de-emphasized things of this world, corroding the foundations of a stratified military society with large-scale waterworks.

Hinayana Buddhism undermined Khmer imperial glory in ways reminiscent of how the Christian cult of simplicity undermined Roman imperial glory (which had included its own bewildering array of gods and temples). In both cases, tribes from the north became increasingly powerful and confident, while decreasingly fertile soils, increasingly exhausted peasants, and decreasingly numerous slaves were less able to generate agricultural surpluses on depleted, ever-drier soil to support the empires and cults. As elsewhere, peasants persist amidst the imperial ruins. As among Italian or Mayan peasants, for instance, parts of the old cosmologies (especially festival calendars) do, too. *Sic transit gloria mundi:* civilizations fall apart. But what a spectacle the twilight of the Khmer Empire offered Zhou Daguan! Even what we can glimpse—which is to say stone and some bronze fragments—inspires awe from late twentieth-century visitors and makes us want to know more than we can about what life was like there eight to ten centuries ago.

Continued ———————————————————————

Burmese as well as for Khmers. Its continuous occupation prevented it from being looted and also held back the jungle.

Glossary

agramahishi — queen who is at the summit (the king's chief wife).

Anavatapta — mythical lake source of the world's rivers (represented by Neak Pean)

Angkor — the various capitals (not just Angkor Thom) between 802 and 1432 and also the name for that period of Khmer history.

Annam — Sinified (rather than Indianized) kingdom in what is now northern Vietnam. The Chinese called it Nan-yüeh, and it is also referred to as Dai-Viet. For a time a province of China, it was able to resist Mongol reconquest.

apsara — celestial dancers/angels.

ashram(a) — Hindu monastery.

avatar — Hindu deity's incarnation.

Ayutthaya — Thai city-kingdom (north of present-day Bangkok) that succeeded Sukhothai (further north) and overran Angkor Thom in 1430-1431.

banteay — citadel.

baray — reservoir.

beng — pond.

bhikshu — Mahayanist Buddhist monk.

bodhisattva — an enlightened future Buddha who, out of compassion, waits to enter *nirvana* in order to save/help others. The most popular in Southeast Asia, Lokeshvara came to be worshipped as a god by Mahayana Buddhists.

Brahma — (Hindu) creator, usually represented with four faces.

chakravartin — sacred universal ruler (*Vrah Kamraten jagat* in Khmer).

Cham — resident of Champa.

Champa — Sanskrit name for the Shivaist kingdom in what is now central Vietnam. The Chinese called it Lin-I. Its capitals were around the modern city of Hué. Champa overran the Khmer Empire in the late twelfth century, and then was conquered by Jayavarman VII. Later it was increasingly dominated by Annam (northern Vietnam). Both its people and its language are called "Cham."

Chenla (Zhenla) — post-Funan, pre-Angkor Khmer kingdom. Chinese sources continued to use this name for the Angkor Khmer Empire.

chen-tan — defloration ceremony described by Zhou Daguan.

chuang — wild bandits (legitimately to be enslaved).

corvée — labor commanded by the state for the construction or repair of roads, temples, etc.

chu-ku — Hinayanist monks (from *chao-ku*).

Dai-Viet — Chinese name for Annam.

devaraja — god-king (*deva* is Sanskrit for "divine," *rajan* for "king"). Originally an incarnation of Shiva, later Khmer kings considered themselves incarnations of Vishnu and Lokeshvara. *Vishnuraja* and *buddharaja* are more appropriate designations for these, but *devaraja* is used as a generic term, not just for Shiva incarnations.

devata — female deity.

dharma — Sanskrit word for "duty," ultimately the duty stemming from one's nature, but also used to refer to duties imposed by laws and customs.

dharmasala — rest house.

Funan — maritime kingdom in what is now southern Cambodia. Angkor Borrei was one of its most important capitals, Oc-Eo its major port.

Ganesha — elephant-faced god who was one of Shiva's generals (and in some accounts, his son as well).

garuda — mythical bird (or bird-head on human trunk) and the mount of Vishnu. Known to be a scourge of snakes.

gopura — temple entrance platform or pavilion.

guru — spiritual advisor.

Harihara — half Vishnu (Hari) and half Shiva (Hara). A number of Khmer statues represent distinct halves.

Hinayana — Northern (Bengal) Buddhism (carried in Pali, though the word is itself Sanskrit, meaning "lesser vehicle"). Also called Theravada, it is the dominant Buddhism of contemporary Southeast Asia.

hotar — royal chaplain (from the Sivakaivalya family between the reign of Jayavarman II and that of Suryavarman I).

jataka — Buddhist stories (often sung and danced).

Isvara — name for Shiva.

jaya — Sanskrit word meaning "victory."

Kailasa — Shiva's mountain-peak home.

kalpa — Sanskrit designation of a cosmic period.

Kambu — mythical ancestor of Kambujas (Cambodians).

Kambuja — Cambodia.

kamrateng jagat — Lord of the universe.

karma — Sanskrit word for "fate," specifically the ethical consequences from earlier lives in the sequence of transmigration/reincarnation.

Khmer — the ethnic majority of Cambodia and also their language. The word is derived from the Arabic "Comar."

kompong — Khmer word for "river port."

Krisha — incarnation of Vishnu.

Laksmi — consort of Vishnu; goddess of beauty, wealth, and happiness.

lingam/linga — usually laterite-porous red sandstone (and sometimes gold-plated) phallic symbol of Shiva (and thereby of his incarnations as Khmer kings), placed at the center of temple-mountains to represent the potency of the *devaraja*.

Lokeshvara — Buddhist *bodhisattva* of mercy (Avalokitshvara) with whom Jayavarman VII identified himself (in the myriad faces smiling in all directions from the Bayon, Angkor Thom gates, etc.). Lokeshvara was assimilated to the cult of Maheshvara, a Hindu deity of compassion, in Southeast Asian Hindu-Buddhist syncretism. In his four arms he carries a lotus, a rosary, a flask, and a book.

Louvo — kingdom centered on what is now the city of Lopburi in central Thailand, that was annexed by Suryavarman I in the late 1020s.

mahanatha — great savior (applied to Jayavarman VII after he defeated the Chams).

Mahayana — Northern (Bengal) Buddhism (carried in Sanskrit, in which it means "great vehicle"). The legitimation of the classic Khmer Empire (and of most of its rivals), it was supplanted by Hinayana/Theravada in Southeast Asia (but not China, Korea, Taiwan, and Japan).

Maitreya — future Buddha.

men — pavilion for burning corpses.

matrilineal — the mother's line (for reckoning genealogy and/or inheritance).

Meru — Hindu mythological mountain supposed to be the center of the universe. Various temples on hills or mountains in themselves (i.e., in their shape) were in effect incarnations of Mount Meru, and the lingam of the *devaraja* in them symbolized his dominance from the center. A belief that the mountain had five peaks led to various five-towered edifices such as Pre Rup, Ta Keo, and Angkor Wat.

Môn — A (derogatory) Chinese term for the inhabitants of Southeast Asia (including the Khmer). Also a language and a kingdom submerged by the Khmer and Tai.

mukhalinga — lingam with a bas-relief head cared on it.

naga — mythological serpent, often multi-headed (much represented as churning the Sea of Milk, and also as the pre-Hinduized Khmer rulers).

nagara — Sanskrit word for "city" (the basis for the Khmer word "Angkor").

Nan-yüeh — Chinese name for Nam Viet. Yüeh referred to
the southern coast of China, and Nan the southern-
most extension. The Chinese called the inhabitants Lo-
yüeh, later Ou-lo, or just Lo.

neak ta — spirits with quite localized power (from rocks,
trees, streams, etc.).

Pancharatra — the South Asian cult of Vishnu.

Parameshvara — "supreme lord" (Shiva, and by extension
his incarnations as Khmer and other Southeast Asian
kings).

Pashupata — the Indian cult of Shiva (from which the no-
tion of *devaraja* derived).

phnom — Khmer word for "hill."

phum — Khmer word for "village," derived from Sanskrit
bhumi, "land."

pradaksina — Sanskrit word for "procession."

prah — sacred.

prasat — tower with a sanctuary (as in each hospital).

preah khan — the sacred sword of state. (Also the temple
northeast of Angkor Thom that Jayavarman VII built
on the site of the victory against the Chams and dedicated to his father Dharanindravarman to whom he
owed his Buddhist faith.)

prei — forest.

primogeniture — inheritance of everything by the oldest
surviving son.

purohita — Shivaist chief priest. Jayavarman II put the family of Sivakaivalya in charge of *devaraja* for eternity—
which lasted until the reign of Suryavarman I.

rajan — Sanskrit word for "king" (from which "royal" is
derived).

Rama — (Hindu) incarnation of Vishnu and hero of the
Ramayana, the great Hindu epic very popular in
Southeast Asia and Indonesia.

rishi — Sanskrit word for ascetic hermit.

sampot — cloth passed between the legs, draped around the hips, and knotted in front.

samrit — bronze, alloy containing some gold and silver.

Shiva — (Hindu) creator and destroyer (often represented with a third eye in the middle of his forehead or as the sacred lingam).

Sinhalese/Singhalese — the Hinayana Buddhist people of Ceylon (now Sri Lanka) and also their language.

srah — pond

sthavira — Hinayanist Buddhist elder.

stupa — Buddhist funerary monument (usually a dome narrowing to a needle above the dome).

ta — Khmer word for "ancestor."

Tai — a language group drifting south from Yunnan into Siam, consolidating control in the Sukhothai and Ayutthaya kingdoms. The latter sacked Angkor Thom in 1430, after which the capital of a much-reduced Khmer kingdom moved from Angkor.

tataka — Sanskrit word for pond/reservoir.

Tambralinga — Tamil-Malay kingdom of Suryavarman I's father, a Khmer dependency throughout the eleventh and twelfth centuries.

Tantrik — mystical Buddhist techniques from the Himalayas (Tibet and Nepal). It may be a partial resurgence of pre-Aryan cults of northeastern India.

Tao — Chinese word for "the way," and associated with (1) the teachings of Lao Tzu, and (2) almost anything that struck medieval Chinese observers as magic, Hinduism in particular. Those the Chinese called "Taoist" in Southeast Asia were not follower of Lao Tzu, but, rather, devotees of Shiva and Vishnu.

Theravada — Pali term meaning "teachings of the elders." This is the common label for Southern (Sri Lankan/Singhalese) Buddhism (carried in Pali rather than Sanskrit). Also called Hinayana, Theravada is the dominant Buddhism of contemporary Southeast Asia (and has been from the fourteen century onward).

Lankan/Singhalese) Buddhism (carried in Pali rather than Sanskrit). Also called Hinayana, Theravada is the dominant Buddhism of contemporary Southeast Asia (and has been from the fourteen century onward).

thom — Khmer word for "large," from Sanskrit *dhama*, grand.

trapeang — Khmer word for "pond" or "pool."

varman — Sanskrit word for "armor." As a suffix of kings' names it meant protector of their people.

vat/wat — Buddhist monastery (and the temple within it).

veda — Sanskrit word for "knowledge." The *Vedas* are various collections of ancient Hindu sacred writings (hymns, prayers, liturgies, exhortations).

Vieng Chan — old name for the capital of Laos (Vientiane more recently).

vihear — Khmer word for "sanctuary."

Vishnu — (Hindu) protector (his four arms hold a disc, a conch shell, a ball, and a club).

wat/vat — Buddhist monastery (and the temple within it).

yaksha — spirit (good or evil).

ya lieh — annual enumeration of the population.

Yashodharapura — the Sanskrit name used for the Khmer capital from 890 to 1451. It is now generally referred to as Angkor Thom (great city).

Yüan — Mongol dynasty of China (1264-1368), successfully resisted by Annam and Angkor, but not by Pagan (Burma).

Zabag — The Arab name for a kingdom of Java, Sumatra, and a considerable part of the Malay peninsula. Its *maharaja*'s decapitation of a Chenla king led the next king, Jayavarman II, to build his capital(s) inland, beginning the Angkor period.

Zhenla (Chenla) — post-Funan, pre-Angkor Khmer kingdom. Chinese sources continued to use this name for the Angkor Khmer Empire.

Profile of one of the Lokeshavaras in the Bayon

Kings of Angkor

Primarily based on dates from Briggs (1951)

King	Dates of Reign	Major Projects Still Visible
Jayavarman II	802-850	Trapean Phong (probably)
Jayavarman III	850-877	
Indravarman I	877-889	Preah Ko, Bakong (Roluos)
Yashovarman I	889-910	Lolei (Roluos)
Harshavarman I	910-?	
Isanavarman II	?-928	Prasat Kravan
Jayavarman IV	928-942	Prasat Thom
Harshavarman II	942-944	
Rajendravarman	944-968	Pre Rup, Eastern Mebon, Banteay Srei
Jayavarman V	968-1001	Ta Keo, Phimeanakas
Udayadityavarman I	1001-1002	
Suryavarman I	1002-1049	
Udayadityavarman II	1050-1065	Baphuon, Prasat Khna
Harshavarman III	1065-1090	Phimai temple
Jayavarman VI	1090-1108	
Dharanindravarman I	1108-1112	Beng Mealea
Suryavarman II	1112-1152	Angkor Wat, Banteay Samré
Harshavarman IV	1152?	
Dharanindravarman II	1152-1160	
Yasovarman II	1160-1165	
Trubuvanadityavarman	1165-1177	(usurper killed by Chams)
Jayavarman VII	1181-1219?	Ta Prohm, Preah Khan, Bayon, Banteay Chmar

King	Dates of Reign	Major Projects Still Visible
Indravarman II	1219?-1243?	
Jayavarman VIII	1243?-1295	
Indravarman III	1295-1307	(Yüan embassy with Zhou Daguan)
Indrajayavarman	1308-1327	
Jayavarman-paramesvara	1327	(last Sanskrit inscription)
	. . .	
Dharmasoka		died during siege of Angkor in 1431
Ponhea Yat		crowned at Angkor is 1432 as Suryavarman, he moved the capital first to Basan, then in 1434 to Phnom Phen; abdicated in 1459

Bibliography

Note: I have included summary books by a number of leading French Indochina scholars. The most recent edition of books in multiple editions is cited. Only seminal articles and/or those quoted or directly drawn upon in the text are included in this bibliography. For specialist articles, see the bibliographies in Briggs (1951) and Hall (1981).

Bagchi, Prabodh Chandra (1929-1930) "On some Tantrik texts studied in Ancient Kambjua." *Indian Historical Quarterly* 5:754-769, 6:97-107.

Bastian, Adolf (1868) *Reise durch Kamboja nach Cochinchina.* Jena: H. Costenoble.

Bechert, Heinz (1973) "Sangha, state, society, 'nation.'" *Dædalus* 102:85-95.

Beylié, Leon Marie Eugene de (1907) *L'architecture hindoue en Extreme-Orient.* Paris: E. Lerous. (Source of drawings on pp. 13, 58, 91.)

Bhattacharya, Kamaleswar (1961) *Les Religions Brahmaniques dans l'ancien Cambodge: d'après l'épigraphie et l'iconographie.* Paris: École Française d'Extrême-Orient.

—— (1991) *Recherches sur le vocabulaire des inscriptions sanskrites du Cambodge.* Paris: École Française d'Extrême-Orient.

Bit, Seanglim (1991) *The Warrior Heritage: A Pscyhological Perspective of Cambodian Trauma.* El Cerrito, CA: Seanglim Bit. (A Cambodian psychologist's reflections on post-traumatic stress, the meanings of the distant past, and Cambodian "national character.")

Boisselier, Jean (1989) *Trends in Khmer Art.* Ithaca, NY: Cornell University Southeast Asia Program.

Bosch, Frederik David Kan (1960) *The Golden Germ: An Introduction to Indian Symbolism.* 's-Gravenhage: Mouton.

Boxer, Charles Ralph (1904) *South China in the Sixteenth Century, Being the Narratives of Galeote Pereira, Father Gaspar da Cruz, O.P. [and] Father Martin de Rada, O.E.S.A. (1550-1575).* London: Hakluyt Society. (Gaspar da Cruz visited post-Angkor Cambodia in 1555-6 and reported Brahmans–not Buddhists! –an insuperable obstacle to proselytizing.)

Briggs, Lawrence Palmer (1948) "Siamese attacks on Angkor before 1430." *Far Eastern Quarterly* 9:3-33.

—— (1951) *The Ancient Khmer Empire.* Philadelphia: American Philosophical Society. (This volume provides the most thorough history in English and a vast bibliography of the mostly-French writings on Angkor buildings and history.)

Chan Moly Sam (1987) *Khmer Court Dance.* Newington, CT: Khmer Studies Institute.

Chatterji, Bijan Raj (1964) *Indian Cultural Influence in Cambodia.* Calcutta: University of Calcutta Press. (First edition 1928. A work of considerable Indian chauvinism.)

Chau Jukua see: Zhao Rugua

Chaudhary, Radhakrishna (1984) *Some Aspects of Social and Economic History of Ancient India and Cambodia.* Delhi: Chaukhambha Orientalia.

Chou Ta-Kuan: see Zhou Daguan

Coe, Michael D. (1961) "Social typology and the tropical forest civilizations." *Comparative Studies in Society and History* 4:65-85. (Coe compares Classic [lowland] Maya and Khmer, arguing that both had huge cult centers rather than true cities, in part because the difficulty of transportation and the uniformity of crops limited trade.)

Coedès, George (1911) "Note sur l'apothéose au Cambodge.' *Bulletin de la Commission Archéolgique Indochinoise* 3:38-49.

—— (1913) "Le serment des fonctionnaires de Suryavarman I." *Bulletin de l'École Française d'Extrême Orient* 13:11-17.

—— (1913) *Le Temple d'Angkor Vat: La galerie des bas-reliefs.* Paris: G. Van Oest (=Publications de l'École française d'Extreme-Orient, Mémoires archeologiques 2, vol. 3). (Source of drawings on pp. 14, 15 21, 30 46, 52.)

—— (1937-1966) *Inscriptions du Cambodge.* Paris: E. de Boccard. (8 volumes.)

—— (1947) *Pour mieux comprendre Angkor.* Paris: Libraire d'Amerique et d'Orient.

—— (1953) "Le substrat autochotone et la superstructure indienne au Cambodge et à Java." *Cahiers d'histoire mondiale* 1,2.

—— (1963) *Angkor: An Introduction.* Hong Kong: Oxford University Press. (Especially notable in this collection of eight brief essays is the one discussing architectural symbolism. There are also sagacious accounts of the pre-Angkor king, Jayavarman II and of Jayavarman VII, and an analysis of personal cults. The French original contains more on changes in French archeological interpretations of Angkor.)

—— (1966) *The Making of South East Asia.* Berkeley: University of California Press. (This synthesis proceeds country by country of mainland Indochina, including Vietnam. The concluding chapter is the best summary of the Indian heritage.)

—— (1968) *The Indianized States of Southeast Asia.* Honolulu: East-West Center Press. (This synthesis is organized by era, juxtaposing what occurred in insular and mainland Hinduized kingdoms of Southeast Asia.)

Commission archeologique de l'Indochine (1910) *Le Bayon d'Angkor Thom: Bas-reliefs.* Paris: E. Leroux. (Source of drawings on pp. 11, 25, 26, 40, 44, 51, 52, 53, 68, 88.)

Coomaraswamy, Ananda K. (1942) *Spiritual Authority and Temporal Power in the Indian Theory of Government.* New Haven, CT: American Oriental Society.

Delvert, Jean (1961) *Le Paysan Cambodgien.* Paris: Mouton.

—— (1983) *Le Cambodge.* Paris: Presses Universitaires de France.

Dufour, Henri, and Charles Carpeaux (1910) *Le Bayon d'Angkor Thom Bas-reliefs.* Paris: Ernest Leroux. (Rare volume containing photographs of the Angkor Thom bas-reliefs.)

Ebihara, May Mayko (1968) *Svay: A Khmer village in Cambodia.* Ph.D. dissertation Columbia University. (Community study of a village before the ensuing chaos of American bombing and Khmer Rouge terror.)

Ferrand, Gabriel (1913-4) *Relations de voyages et de textes géographiques arbas, persans et turcs relatives à l'Extréme-Orient du VIIIᵉ au XVIIᵉ siècles.* Paris: Ernest Leroux. (A two-volume collection of texts by Muslims relating to East and Southeast Asia.)

Finot, Louis (1925) "Lokeçvara en Indochine." *Études Asiatiques* 1:227-256.

—— (1927) *L'origine d'Angkor.* Phnom-Penh: A. Portail.

—— (1956) *Le bouddhisme: son origine, son évolution.* Phnom-Penh: Editions de l'Institut bouddhique.

Frédéric, Louis (1981) *La Vie Quotidienne dans la Péninsule Indochinoise a l'époque d'Angkor.* Paris: Hachette.

Giteau, Madeleine (1966) *Khmer Sculpture and the Angkor Civilization.* New York: Abrams.

—— (1976) *The Civilization of Angkor.* New York: Rizzoli.

Ghosh, Manomohan (1968) *A History of Cambodia from the Earliest Time to the End of the French Protectorate.* Calcutta: Oriental Book Agency. (A provocative, revisionist history.)

Goloubew, Victor (1924) "L'hydralique urbaine et agricola à l'époque des rois d'Angkor." *Cahiers de l'École Française d'Extrême-Orient* 24:16-19.

Gorgoniev, Urii Aleksandrovich (1966) *The Khmer Language.* Moscow: Nauka Publishing House.

Groslier, Bernard-Philippe (1958) *Angkor et le Cambodge au XVIᵉ siècle d'après les sources portugaises et espagnoles.* Paris: Presses Universitaires de France. (A collection of the first European observations of post-Angkor Cambodia.)

—— (1960) "Our knowledge of the Khmer civilization: a reappraisal." *Journal of The Siam Society* 48:1-28. (In addition to reporting on archaeological projects, particularly excavation of the Phimeanakas, G provides the crispest judgement of the the extent and limits of Indian influence on Angkor-era civilization.)

—— (1966) *Angkor: Art and Civilization.* New York: Praeger.

Groslier, George (1921) *Recherches sur les Cambodgiens*. Paris: A. Challamel.

—— (1933) *Angkor*. Paris: Librairie Renouard, H. Laurens.

Hall, Daniel George Edward (1981) *A History of South-East Asia*. London: Macmillan Press.

Heine-Geldern, Robert von (1930) "Weltbild und Bauform in Südostasien." *Weiner Beiträge zur Kunst und Kultur Asiens* 4:28-78. Issued in English as *Conceptions of State and Kingship in Southeast Asia*. Ithaca, NY: Cornell University Southeast Asia Program, 1968. (A brief, but very discerning synthesis.)

Higham, Charle (1989) The Archaeology of Mainland Southeast Asia from 10,000 B.C. to the Fall of Angkor. New York: Cambridge University Press.

Jacq-Hergoualc'h, Michel (1979) *L'armement et l'organisation de larmée khmere: aux XIIe et XIIIe siecles: d'apres les bas-reliefs d'Angkor Vat, du Bayon et de Banteay Chmar*. Paris: Presses universitaires de France.

Lévi, Sylvain (1928) *L'Inde et le Monde*. Paris: H. Champion.

Lingat, Robert (1952-1955) *Les régimes matrimoniaux du sud-est de l'Asie*. Paris: E. de Boccard. (2 vol.)

Ma Touan-Lin (1883 [1273]) *Ethnographie des peuples étrangers a la Chine*. Paris: Ernest Leroux. (See vol. II:436-444 on Funan, 476-488 on "Tchinla." Translated from *Ssu i k'ao* and annotated by d'Hervey de Saint Denys. The most accessible edition of the Chinese text is *Wen hsien tung kao*, Taipei: Taiwan shang wu yin shu kuan, 1983.)

Majumdar , R. C. (1944) *Kabuja-desa*. Madras: University of Madras.

Mouhot, Henri (1966[1858-1861]) *Diary: Travels in the Central Parts of Siam, Cambodia, and Laos During the Years 1858-61*. Kuala Lumpur: Oxford University Press. (Abridged and edited by Christopher Pym. Mouhout was the modern European rediscover of Angkor, which had already been mentioned in seventeenth-century Spanish writings.)

Murray, Stephen O. (1994) "A thirteenth-century imperial ethnography." *Anthropology Today* 10,5:15-18. (Discussion of the similarities between Zhou Daguan and European colonial anthropologists of the twentieth century. A major difference is that Zhou included discussion of the place of his countrymen.)

Mus, Paul (1935) *Barabudur: esquisse d'une histoire du bouddhisme fondée sur la critique archeologique des textes.* Hanoi: Impr. d'Extreme-Orient.

Myrdal, Jan (1970) *Angkor: An Essay on Art and Interpretation.* New York: Pantheon. (Cranky essay on racism with unsubstantiated claims that peasants became poorer with the increase of rice production made possible by irrigation. Accompanied by atmospheric black-and-white photographs by Gun Kessle.)

Pelliot, Paul (1903) "Fou-nan." *Bulletin de l'École Française d'Extrême Orient* 3:248-303.

—— (1925) "Quelques textes chinois concernant l'Indochine hindouisée.'" *Études Asiatiques* 2:243-263.

Porée, Guy, and Eveline Maspero (1938) *Mours et coutumes des Khmers.* Paris: Payot.

Porée-Maspero, Eveline (1962-1964) *Étude sur les rites agraires des Cambodgiens.* Paris: Mouton. (3 volumes.)

Pym, Christopher (1968) *The Ancient Civilization of Angkor.* New York: Mentor. (A generally excellent, but occasionally annoying, introduction to Khmer history and culture.)

Sankalia, Hasmukhlal Dhirajlal (1972) *The University of Nalanda.* Delhi: Oriental Publishers.

Schiller, Eric (1996) "Khmer Writing" in *The World's Writing Systems,* ed. Peter T. Daniels and Bill Bright, pp. 467-473. New York: Oxford University Press.

Sharan, Mahesh Kumar (1981) *Select Cambodian Inscriptions: The Mebon and Pre Rup Inscriptions of Rajendra Varman II.* Delhi: S.N. Publications.

Stierlin, Henri (1984) *The Cultural History of Angkor.* London: Aurum.

Sirafi, Abu Zayd Hasan ibn Yazid (1922[916]) *Voyage du marchand arabe Sulayman en Inde et en Chine, rédigé en 851.* Paris: Editions Bossard.

Srivastava, Krishna Murari (1987) *Angkor Wat and Cultural Ties with India.* New Delhi: Books & Books.

Stern, Philippe (1927) *Le Bayon d'Angkor et l'évolution de l'art khmer.* Paris, P. Geuthner.

—— (1934) "Le temple-montagne khmèr: la culte du linga et la devaraja." *Bulletin de l'École Française d'Extrême Orient* 38:150-173.

Stierlin, Henri (1984) *The Cultural History of Angkor.* London: Aurum Press.

Tambiah, Stanley Jeyaraja (1973) "The persistence and transformation of tradition in Southeast Asia." *Dædalus* 102:55-84.

—— (1987) *The Buddhist Conception of Universal King and its Manifestations in South and Southeast Asia.* Kuala Lumpur: University of Malaya.

Wales, Horace Geoffrey Quaritch (1953) *The Mountain of God: A Study in Early Religion and Kingship.* London: Bernard Quaritch. (Argues for a prominent pre-Hindu "megalithic" stratum of earth god rather than sky god worship across Asia, stressing that Khmer temple mountains were more than Hindu towers.)

—— (1965) *Angkor and Rome: A Historical Comparison.* London: Bernard Quaritch. (A natural history of the two empires with a somewhat inordinate stress on civic religion, but a corrective of interpretations crediting everything Khmer to India. Wales shows that while "the Khmers and Romans initially benefitted much from what they had learnt from India or Greece, almost all that they accomplished in their periods of greatness was after they had thrown off the later influences [Tantrism and Dionysianism] of their now-declining mentors, and found new strength in their own spirit and deep-seated traditions" [p. xvii].)

—— (1974) *The Making of Greater India.* London: Bernard Quaritch.

Wheatcroft, Rachel (1928) *Siam and Cambodia in Pen and Pastel, with Excursions in China and Burmah.* London, Constable & Co. (Source of drawings on pp. 9, 107.)

Wolters, O. W. (1982) *History, Culture, and Region in Southeast Asian Perspectives.* Singapore: Institute of Southeast Asian Studies.

Young, Ernest (1898)*The Kingdom of the Yellow Robe,* London: Archibald Constable.

Zhou Daguan [Chou Ta-Kuan] (1992 [1297]) *The Customs of Cambodia.* Bangkok: Siam Society. (Translated into English by J. Paul from the 1902 French translation of Paul Pelliot in *Bulletin de l'École Française d'Extrême Orient* 2 (1902):123-177, without Pelliot's notes. The most accessible edition of the Chinese text is *Chen-la feng tu chi,* Taipei: Taiwan shang wu yin shu kuan, 1983. This is the closest thing to an ethnography that exists of Khmer civilization already in its twilight. It is the primary basis for everything written about life in Angkor, not least the present volume.)

Zhou Rugua [Chau Jukua] (1911 [1225]) *A Description of Barbarous Peoples: Chinese and Arab Trade in the Twelfth and Thriteenth Centuries, Entitled Chu-fan-chi.* St. Petersburg: Imperial Academy of Sciences. (Translated and extensively annotated by Friedrich Hirth and W. W. Rockhill. The most accessible edition of the Chinese text is *Shang hsia chuan,* Taipei: Taiwan shang wu yin shu kuan, 1984.)

Index

Bolded pages-number entries refer to major topics; page numbers in *italics* refer to the glossary on page 136.